Resilience of the Soul

Resilience of the Soul

Developing Emotional and Spiritual Resilience in Adolescents and Their Families

A program and resource guide
for congregations based on the
Kedushat HaGuf program

Written and Compiled
by Rabbi Edythe Held Mencher, LCSW
with Yael Shmilovitz and Rabbi Michael Howald

With introduction by Rabbi Richard F. Address, D.Min

URJ Press
Department of Jewish Family Concerns
Union for Reform Judaism
New York, New York

**Union for Reform Judaism
Department of Jewish Family Concerns
Phone: (212) 650-4294   Fax: (212) 650-4239
E-mail: JFC@urj.org   Web site: www.urj.org/jfc**

Jean Abarbanel, Chair

Mike Grunebaum, Vice-chair

Carole Sterling, Vice-chair

Linda Wimmer, Vice-chair

Michael P. Friedman, Chair of *Kedushat HaGuf* Committee

For permission to reprint, please contact URJ Press at:

URJ Press
633 Third Avenue
New York, NY 10017-6778

(212) 650-4124
press@urj.org

Library of Congress Cataloging-in-Publication Data
Mencher, Edythe Held.
   Resilience of the soul : developing emotional and spiritual resilience in adolescents and their
families : a program and resource guide for congregations based on the kedushat ha guf program /
written and compiled by Edythe Held Mencher with Yael Shmilovitz and Michael Howald.
       p.   cm
   Includes bibliographical references.
   ISBN-13: 978-0-8074-1064-6 (pbk. : alk. paper)
   ISBN-10: 0-8074-1064-0 (pbk. : alk. paper)
   1. Jewish teenagers—North America—Conduct of life. 2. Jewish teenagers—North America—
Pastoral counseling of. 3. Resilience (Personality trait) in adolescence. 4. Resilience (Personality
trait)—Religious aspects—Judaism. 5. Mental health—Religious aspects—Judaism. 6. Parent and
teenager—Religious aspects—Judaism. 7. Jewish teenagers—North America—Conduct of life—
Problems, exercises, etc. 8. Jewish families—North America—Prayers and devotions. I. Shmilovitz, Yael.
II. Howald, Michael. III. Title
   BM727.M46 2007
   296.70835—dc22   2007030006

© 2007 by URJ Press
This book is printed on acid-free paper.

Manufactured in the United States of America

10 9 8 7 6 5 4 3 2 11

Contents

Permissions

Every attempt has been made to obtain permission to reprint previously published material. The authors gratefully acknowledge the following for permission to reprint previously published material:

CENTRAL CONFERENCE OF AMERICAN RABBIS: Excerpt from *Gates of Prayer: The New Union Prayerbook: Weekdays, Sabbaths, and Festivals Services and Prayers for Synagogue and Home.* Copyright © 1975 by Central Conference of American Rabbis. By permission of the Central Conference of American Rabbis.

CROSSCURRENTS MAGAZINE: Excerpt from "Liturgies in Anger" by David Blumenthal in *Cross Currents Magazine* Vol. 52, No. 2. Copyright © by CrossCurrents magazine. Reprinted by permission of the publisher.

CURTIS BROWN, LTD.: Copyright © 1996 by Harold Kushner. First published in *How Good Do We Have To Be?* by Harold Kushner. Reprinted by permission of Curtis Brown, Ltd.

HOWARD SCHWARTZ: "Isaac" by Haim Gouri. Translation copyright © 1980 by Howard Schwartz. Used by permission of Howard Schwartz.

JEWISH LIGHTS: Excerpt from *Sacred Intentions: Daily Inspiration to Strengthen the Spirit, Based on Jewish Wisdom* © 1999 Rabbi Kerry M. Olitzky and Rabbi Lori Forman (Woodstock, VT: Jewish Lights Publishing). $15.95+$3.95 s/h. Order by mail or call 800-962-4544 or on-line at **www.jewishlights.com** Permission granted by Jewish Lights Publishing, P.O. Box 237, Woodstock, VT 05091; Excerpt from *Lifecycles V. 2: Jewish Women on Biblical Themes in Contemporary Life* © 1997 Debra Orenstein and Jane Rachel Litman. $19.95+$3.95 s/h. Order by mail or call 800-962-4544 or on-line at **www.jewishlights. com** Permission granted by Jewish Lights Publishing, P.O. Box 237, Woodstock, VT 05091

OXFORD UNIVERSITY PRESS: Excerpt (300 words) from p. 238 from *Gabriel's Palace: Jewish Mystical Tales* by Howard Schwartz (1994). Copyright © 1993 by Howard Schwartz. By permission of Oxford University Press, Inc.

RANDOM HOUSE, INC: From *Talking to God* by Naomi Levy, copyright © 2002 by Naomi Levy. Used by permission of Alfred A. Knopf, a division of Randon House, Inc.

Introduction

It is with great pleasure that the Department of Jewish Family Concerns of the Union for Reform Judaism presents to you *Resilience of the Soul*. This resource, program, and study guide is the result of two years worth of pilot workshops, seminars, discussions, and encounters with adolescents, parents, congregations, camps, youth workers, and clergy. Emerging from the Department's project *Kedushat HaGuf* (Holiness of the Body), *Resilience of the Soul* is designed to help facilitate and guide discussions and programs with the Jewish community that seek to validate, dignify, and honor individuals and families who have had to deal with challenging and stressful emotions and situations. None of us are immune to such situations, and when these involve adolescents and parents, the emotions and concerns are often magnified. How do we bring these issues into discussion within our congregations, camps, and youth groups? How do we surround these discussions within a context that affirms the fundamental value that each of us is in "the image of God"? *Resilience of the Soul* has been designed to help answer these questions from a foundation of caring, honor, respect, and love. It seeks to validate the reality that every one of us and every one of our families often finds themselves in the "wilderness."

The evolution of the *Kedushat HaGuf* project showed us that the most meaningful approach to dealing with many of the challenging issues that face adolescents and their families in the contemporary North American culture is to base our discussions in the powerful truths and interpretations that are rooted in Jewish texts. To that end, you will find some very relevant examples of how to use classic texts in dealing with sensitive issues. These texts, and the programs that accompany them, have been modeled in various venues: in congregations, URJ camps, and meetings. Dozens of individuals, clergy, families, teachers, and professionals have helped shape this resource. Their stories have added to the collective experience that has brought this book into your hands.

Why create this book? The answer to that question rests with the reason for the contemporary synagogue. If we do not respond in caring and supportive ways to the needs and realities of our families, then we court the danger of being made marginal to our people in times of need. The strength of the synagogue is its ability to create a caring community, and to do that means that we must bring the power and message of our tradition and texts to the struggles and challenges of everyday life.

The exploration of the issues confronted in this book grew from the Department's original project on eating disorders. That project, *Litapayach Tikvah* (To Nourish Hope), began to shed light on behaviors that were impacting adolescents and thus, their families. These discussions were followed by sessions with the URJ Camp, Youth, and Life Long Learning

staffs. There, we learned that there was a host of self destructive behaviors that were showing up within our youth groups, camps, and congregations. What was asked of us was to see
if we could create text-based responses and programs that would allow our communities to
begin to address these issues from a nonjudgmental, nonpathological perspective. If we were
to model the value of being a caring community, we could not ignore these realities; rather
we had to accept the challenge of how to introduce these difficult issues into the conversations of our community. The leadership of the Department accepted this challenge and
the journey began.

There are many people who have contributed to this project and this book. Hundreds of
our own young people filled out surveys and were involved in pilot programs and workshops. URJ regional directors scheduled sessions at their regional conventions and dozens
of congregations agreed to hold sessions. Our departmental chairperson, Jean Abarbanel,
along with Vice-chairs Linda Wimmer, Mike Grunebaum, and Carole Sterling, supported
the creation of a lay team that helped guide and shape the project. Michael Freidman
chaired that group and continues to lead the effort to expand the project. Rabbi Lisa Izes,
who was Assistant Director of Jewish Family Concerns at the time we began this project,
added insight and her own dedication as our work began. We have received wonderful support in much of this work from the Union Camp system. Paul Reichenbach and Lisa David
opened the door to several of our camps so that we could create pilot sessions for staff and
campers. The challenging nature of much of this work has received continuing support
from the URJ professional leadership and we specifically thank Rabbi Elliott Kleinman,
Director of Programming.

Nothing would have been possible, however, without the financial support of David (*z'l*)
and Shirley Toomim of Houston, Texas. Their foundation provided the seed money that
allowed us to develop material and programs and to test that material in venues all around
North America. The lives that have already been touched by these discussions would not
have been except for the foresight and commitment of the Toomim family. Likewise,
Women for Reform Judaism came forward to assist us with additional financial support for
our work. WRJ has consistently seen the value in dealing with difficult issues within the
framework of the congregation and has assisted our department in many ways.

Ideas, programs, and resources by themselves are fine. For them to begin to have impact,
however, they need to be organized, shaped, and given definition. The Department of
Jewish Family Concerns has been blessed to have two individuals who devoted countless
hours to the development, shaping, and evolving of this project. Rabbi Michael Howald
(Hebrew Union College–New York 2006) was our departmental intern in 2005–2006. He
was present at the creation of what was *Kedushat HaGuf* and was instrumental in writing
and researching the foundations of *Resilience of the Soul*. Yael Shmilovitz (Hebrew Union
College–New York 2008) succeeded Rabbi Howald as intern for 2006–2007. Yael's gifts,
passion, and talents are evident throughout this book. Her dedication to the completion of
the book is greatly appreciated. Yael's unique insights into the changes we were noticing as
we continued to develop the project added immeasurably to the revisioning of some of our
essential messages and texts. Likewise, Dessa Shepherd, our administrative assistant, worked
with us all in helping draft countless documents and tabulate hundreds of surveys. URJ
Press has been, as usual, a friend and supporter of this and many of our projects and a special thank you must go to Rabbi Hara Person and Ron Ghatan.

Resilience of the Soul includes a variety of resources and links that have helped inform its
development. Part of the excitement of creating this project has been the number of indi-

viduals and organizations that have become known to us. One, however, needs special thanks. Dennis Gilbert, of the URJ North American Board and a member of the Jewish Family Concerns committee, created the linkage between our department and the major center in Israel that deals with trauma related issues. That linkage has evolved into a close relationship, and materials from the center have been adapted for inclusion in *Resilience of the Soul.* For their generosity in allowing us to use their wonderful materials in our guide, and for sharing their time and expertise with us both in visits to Israel and via phone and e-mail over the Atlantic, we express our deepest gratitude and appreciation to Dr. Naomi Baum and the *Temmy and Albert Latner Israel Center for the Treatment of Psychotrauma at Herzog Hospital in Jerusalem, Israel.* Our partnership in helping those who are hurt, be it in Israel or in North America, fills us with great satisfaction and inspires us to continue on this important task.[1]

Rabbi Mencher and I would like to extend our heartfelt gratitude to Rabbi Mencher's colleagues and friends, Ann Engelland, MD (whose specialty is adolescent medicine) and Elizabeth Cohn Stuntz, LCSW (whose specialty is adolescent psychotherapy). Each served as a consultant; each helped to craft a vision of what is most helpful to adolescents and their families, bringing a sense of the spiritual, of what contributes to emotional and physical health, and of how to easily and openly speak with teens about difficult topics. Their generosity in sharing their time and expertise, their participation in conferences in New York and the URJ Biennial in Houston, their willingness to review material, and their ongoing support and belief in the importance of this project have had a profound influence on the work and on the guidebook.

The soul of the project and, indeed, this book, belongs to the dedicated presence of our associate director, Rabbi Edythe Mencher. Rabbi Mencher took on the responsibility of heading up the *Kedushat HaGuf* project and brought her unique insights as rabbi and clinician to bear on the project and this volume. Her tireless efforts to work with congregations, families, and individuals, to help shape their experiences and their stories, have uplifted many and inspired even more. In the process of creating this resource and program book, Rabbi Mencher has helped individuals and families to see the strength and power of a sacred and caring community and has shown congregations and leadership how texts can be used to shed light on the struggles and challenges that so often are present within our families and are so often ignored.

Resilience of the Soul is filled with important and powerful lessons, ideas, and tools. It is a rich how-to volume on engaging congregations and families in discussions about serious and difficult issues. The format has been designed to allow you to pick and choose and shape these discussions in a variety of ways that can reflect the specific needs of your community. What we ask of you is that you begin the conversation. Dare to risk engaging your young people in what is impacting their lives. Be challenged to speak to parents about their own needs and seek to create possible opportunities for generations to be brought together to learn from each other, be strengthened by each other, and be embraced by a community of faith and tradition. None of the program suggestions within this book are simple. They require some strength and courage. Yet, these are our young people, our families, and our

---

[1]For further information and materials contact the *Temmy and Albert Latner Israel Center for the Treatment of Psychotrauma at Herzog Hospital in Jerusalem*: **www.traumaweb.org, traumacenter@herzoghospital.com**; tel: 972-2-6782899, fax: 972-2-6789908

communities that we are speaking to and with and about. We welcome your engagement of discussions and action.

Shalom,
Rabbi Richard F. Address, D.Min
Director, URJ Department of Jewish Family Concerns

Opening Meditation on *Resilience of the Soul*

Be with my child, and hear his cries, wherever he is

Early next morning, Abraham got up and took bread and a waterskin and handed them to Hagar, placing them and the boy on her shoulder. Then he cast her out; trudging away, she wandered aimlessly in the wilderness of Beersheba. When the water in the skin was all gone, she cast the child away under a bush; she walked away and sat down on the other side at a remove of about a bowshot, thinking: "Let me not see the child's death." There, on the other side, she sat and wept in a loud voice.

God heard the boy's cry, and from heaven an angel of God called to Hagar and said,

אַל־תִּירְאִי כִּי־שָׁמַע אֱלֹהִים אֶל־קוֹל הַנַּעַר בַּאֲשֶׁר הוּא־שָׁם:

"What is troubling you, Hagar? Have no fear, for God has heard the cry of the lad where he is. Get up, lift the boy, and hold him with your hand, for I am going to make of him a great nation." God then opened her eyes, and she saw a well. She went and filled the skin with water and gave the boy to drink.

God was with the boy, and he grew up.

—Genesis 21:14–20

Despite all that had happened to her and all she has lost, Hagar believes the voice of an angel that insists that she should not give up, that she should take her son's hand and go on. The angel's words open her eyes and she sees a well of living water where before she had seen nothing but desert. The pain of Abraham receding in the distance isn't gone, but her child drinks enough so that they both can go on living, knowing that even in the driest places, this world contains springs and those who can lead us to them.

Who or what is the angel that spoke to Hagar? What are angels? What difference do they make? The word for angel in Hebrew, *malach*, is also the word for messenger. The Bible suggests that angels do appear in human form as messengers of God. There are people who at first seem unremarkable, who may even be strangers to those in whose lives they emerge to play a momentary or more enduring role. They are the ones who soften the blows that life brings to bear upon us; the ones who affirm that the human cry does not go unheeded; and the people who remind us that we are worth comforting, worth sheltering, worth encouraging. Judaism proposes that those who carry this message truly are angels.

Hagar desperately needs such an angel. Hagar is like every distraught parent who has used up all of the resources he or she has to sustain her child and cannot bear to look on as he suffers and his life and vitality drain away. Just when it appears that all is lost, God hears the cry of the child where he is and an angel appears who makes it possible for Hagar to find the sources of nourishment that exist even in the desert. So many parents find themselves desperate to help their children but without any sense of where to turn—they find themselves looking on helplessly as drugs, eating disorders, alcohol abuse, depression, and self-inflicted violence distort and endanger their child's life. Such circumstances call upon us to assume the role of angels, the messengers of God, who let these parents know that they are not alone, that their cries and those of their children have been heard, and that we will help them to find the sources of help that will sustain them and their children. None of us need feel that we are wandering alone in the desert as long as others in our community can become messengers of God capable of leading us to sources of help. The Union for Reform Judaism offers *Resilience of the Soul* as a way of helping all of us to become the messengers, to hear the cry, and to open the eyes of those who suffer so that they can see the sources of help that exist in our world.

How to Use This Book

Below you will find some suggestions on how to find your way around this book.

❏ *If you are just trying to get a feel of what this book is all about:*
- Section 1:
  Step-by-Step Guide to *Resilience of the Soul* (page 3)
- Section 2:
  What Is Resilience? (page 17)
  Coping in Ways That Hurt Us (page 27)
  Some Things Your Congregation Can Do *Now* to Help Encourage Resilience
  (page 39)

❏ *If a situation is brought to you where self-destructive behaviors are involved:*
- Section 2:
  What Is Resilience? (page 17)
  Coping in Ways That Hurt Us (page 27)
  Suicide Prevention (page 35)
- Section 5:
  Suggestions for When You Want to Hurt Yourself (page 147)

❏ *If you are gathering information about what's going on in your community:*
- Section 1:
  Step-by-Step Guide to *Resilience of the Soul* (page 3)
- Section 2:
  What Is Resilience? (page 17)
  Coping in Ways That Hurt Us (page 27)
  Some Things Your Congregation Can Do *Now* to Help Encourage Resilience
  (page 39)
- Section 4:
  Surveys for Teens, Staff, and Parents (page 87)

❏ *If you are writing a sermon:*
- Section 1:
  Sample *D'var Torah* to Introduce the Program (page 11)

- Section 2:

  What Is Resilience? (page 17)

  Coping in Ways That Hurt Us (page 27)

  Some Things Your Congregation Can Do *Now* to Help Encourage Resilience (page 39)

- Section 3: Text Studies (page 41)
- Section 6: Meditations, Inspirational Readings, and Prayers (page 149)

❑ *If you are creating a worship service:*

- Section 6: Meditations, Inspirational Readings, and Prayers (page 149)

❑ *If you are planning a workshop for teens, parents, or both:*

Information and initial planning

- Section 1:

  Step-by-Step Guide to *Resilience of the Soul* (page 3)

  Sample *D'var Torah* to Introduce the Program (page 11)

  Sample Letter to Parents (page 7)

- Section 2:

  What Is Resilience? (page 17)

  Coping in Ways That Hurt Us (page 27)

  Suicide Prevention (page 35)

- Section 3: Text Studies (page 41)
- Section 4:

  Best Practices 1: Sample Program Materials from Temple Sinai of Toronto (page 67)

  Best Practices 2: Sample Program Materials from Congregation Rodef Shalom in Pittsburgh (page 73)

  Outline: Session for Parents and Synagogue Professionals on Resiliency (page 81)

For program ideas and exercises

- Section 4:

  Teen Survey (page 88)

  Parent Survey (page 97)

- Section 5:

  How We Eat (page 105)

  What Helps and What Doesn't: Ruth Versus Elkanah (page 117)

  Exercises for Expressing Emotions and Coping with Fear (page 121)

  Creating Your Own Blessing (page 129)

  Relaxation Techniques (page 131)

  Exercises for Making Meaning and Finding Hope for the Future (page 137)

  Keeping a Creative Journal (page 143)

- Section 6:

  Creating a Shelter of Peace (page 151)

❑ *If you are planning a training session for staff*

For information and initial planning

- Section 1:

  Step-by-Step Guide to *Resilience of the Soul* (page 3)

Congregational Response to the Needs of Adolescents, Young Adults, and Their Families:
How to Begin

Step-by-Step Guide to *Resilience of the Soul*

1. **Take a deep breath and relax.** No doubt you and your staff strive daily to make your synagogue a safe and sheltering space for teens, as you accompany them on their maturation process toward becoming healthy, confident, ethical, and contributing adult members of society. As we all know, this is a journey that can sometimes be tumultuous, and all of us—teens, parents, teachers, and friends—sometimes need support and guidance along the way. Perhaps you and/or your staff have already been approached privately about at least some of the challenges and concerns relating to teens' lives discussed in this resource guide. Perhaps you have already been wondering how you can better integrate approaches that teach kids how to develop emotional resilience. The URJ Department of Jewish Family Concerns (JFC) wants to help you educate yourself, your staff, and your congregation about the ways in which your congregation can live up to its full potential as a safe space for all, where both successes and challenges can be discussed on a congregational basis in a constructive and caring way. In Jewish tradition certain prayers are meant to be said in public and not in solitary; so it is with the difficult journeys of one's life: no one is meant to walk them alone. With your assistance and the resources provided by JFC, we are developing materials and programming to help to strengthen our adolescents, young adults, and ourselves to cope with the pressures of growing up and living in the twenty-first century.

2. **Begin an initial conversation with staff about why and how the congregation might benefit from integrating resilience-building approaches and addressing the issues brought up in this guide.** Some people will question whether the youngsters and families in your community feel concern about their ability to manage pressures. An initial conversation, then, should include an internal assessment of the challenges and concerns the congregation would benefit most from discussing, based on the experience of staff from interactions with parents and adolescents. We also recommend this initial discussion be held in a group setting so everyone can share their perceptions. This is because so often specific worrisome behaviors, incidents, or concerns have been handled quietly through private discussions with parents and clergy, and there is little sense of how frequently problems have been encountered.

3. **Begin to assess the needs of the community through conversations with members of the congregation, including both parents and children.** Assemble an initial

task force of staff and members—including clergy and mental health professionals as well as parents and teens. This group will be responsible for creating awareness of issues affecting teens and parents, assessing needs, and creating initial programming. Keep in mind that meetings focused on specific behaviors are probably not helpful at this stage of the process. Instead, we recommend meetings designed to elicit parental and adolescent wisdom about what's really happening in the community and what they think the staff needs, or needs to know, to begin to address these issues on a congregational basis. Remember, also, that initial programs/meetings entitled "Parenting Your Jewish Adolescent" or "Teaching Resilience to Our Youth" will have more success than "What to Do If Your Teenager Is a Binge Drinker." Consider some of the following issues:

- What are some of the needs and concerns experienced by teens and parents in the community? Make use of surveys and discussion guides available through JFC, which will enable you to gather information concerning the areas in which teens and parents would like to have more choices and support, and the ways in which teens and parents presently manage the sometimes extraordinarily stressful situations in their lives.

- What sort of communal resources currently exist in order to respond to the needs of teens and their parents? For example, does the synagogue's youth group offer a less competitive, more accepting environment than the one they find at school? Do opportunities exist for youth to build a sense of competence and self worth through making meaningful contributions to society?

We recommend that the congregation have meetings for teens and parents together, but also provide an opportunity for adolescents to express themselves on these issues in a safe and judgment-free environment separate from their parents.

4. **Once the congregation has determined the areas of concern and importance for your unique community, it should begin to craft a meaningful response.** You might wish to consider these factors:

- Does the congregation already have committees or groups that might accept responsibility for implementing various programs and resources from this guide? If not, does the congregation need to develop new committees or groups for this program?

- Does the congregation already have members who have expertise on adolescence, stress management, and building resilience, either from their professional lives or personal experiences? Consider involving them in planning and implementing programs.

- When (what grade or grades) does the congregation intend to provide these programs?

- How (through what type of educational forums) should the congregations provide this information? Does the congregation already have programs and events where approaches that encourage resilience can be integrated? For example, you may want to think in terms of preexisting parent-child workshops, which can be ideal for promoting positive communication, validating children's emotions, and helping them to cope effectively and safely. Venues like the religious school, *b'nei mitzvah* retreats, youth groups, etc., can be strengthened to function as safe spaces where members are helped and guided to speak respectfully and compassionately to each other; these spaces need to be reenvisioned as spaces that are secure enough to let negative emotion be tolerated, as well as responded to in a constructive and caring manner.

- Who (what mixture of staff, other professionals, and lay leadership) should present the information?
- How will staff be trained to work with *Resilience of the Soul?*

5. **Contact JFC.** Let us assist you to develop a program tailored to your congregation's assessment of its needs. We can provide you with materials and resources to address each of the issues your congregation found most pressing. We can also help coordinate your efforts with other congregations in your area.

6. **Contact your regional director.** Your regional director can inform you about what other congregations have developed in terms of resources and programming. Your regional director can also help coordinate your efforts with other nearby synagogues.

7. **Don't forget the long-term perspective.** We hope *Resilience of the Soul* brings positive change to your synagogue and community. With this resource guide we aim to increase resilience and promote wholeness not just in the lives of teens but in our synagogue culture at large.

Rabbi Elazar ben Azaryah teaches us in the Mishnah about a tree whose branches may be few but whose roots are many; even if all the winds in the world come and blow against it, it cannot be felled. When we create a Jewish community—when we teach and learn resilience; when we offer support and comfort through texts, meditations, and prayers; when we build strong friendships through shared activities and communal endeavors—we are setting sturdy Jewish roots. It is those strong Jewish roots that will enable us and our kids to draw sustenance, and find strength and wholeness, so that we can withstand the stormy times in our lives.

Sample Letter to Parents

This is a sample letter to introduce Resilience of the Soul *to parents and to invite their participation. While encouraging parent participation, the letter stresses that the program has the potential to be helpful to their kids whether or not their kids participate. Of course, you should adapt this letter to describe the actual programs and issues of focus chosen by your congregation.*

Dear Parent,

We want to inform you of an important new initiative our synagogue has decided to engage in aimed at better supporting our teens and their families.

We will be implementing this initiative, entitled *Resilience of the Soul*, in collaboration with the Department of Jewish Family Concerns of the Union for Reform Judaism.

Our goal is to enhance our kids' resilience (and not only theirs, but that of their entire family!) as they deal with the trials of adolescence and young adulthood. We believe that resilience is indeed a learned skill; it is the idea that we can be taught to manage life's challenges in ways that promote health and wholeness.

We know that adolescence is a difficult period for kids, and no less for their parents. This is exactly the reason why we want to make sure Temple _____ is a place where both teens and parents can draw spiritual and emotional sustenance in the face of challenges and uncertainties, as well as share their joys and accomplishments.

At this stage we are beginning to plan facilitated discussions for staff, parents, and teens designed to help families explore issues such as managing pressures and self-care, as well as to encourage them to see the synagogue as a place to find understanding and guidance. Topics include ways of dealing with cultural demand for perfection, ways of handling strong emotions, ways of reaching out and helping someone in distress, and moderation in eating and drinking.

We are not engaging in a therapeutic initiative, rather, we want to expand the boundaries of conversation here at Temple _____. We believe that the synagogue is among the few places where the community can address these issues in a safe and caring Jewish environment.

While our synagogue cannot offer therapy, it *can* offer our young people and families a place in which they can draw upon human and spiritual sources of affirmation, cooperation, acceptance, and hope.

We have decided to begin integrating resilience-building approaches into the synagogue because we know that the pressures and pitfalls of adolescence, from middle school through college, are very real. We believe that with your help and support we can make a difference in the lives of our young people and their families.

We strongly encourage your participation. We think the involvement of all generations can make a meaningful change by letting our young people know that they have our love and support, and enabling them to experience themselves as worthwhile and cherished. Whether you can be here or not, we invite you to be in touch with _____ if you have any questions.

We have planned a meeting on _____. Please respond to _____ to let us know whether you will be able to attend.

Sample Letter to Staff

Dear Staff Member,

We have scheduled a meeting for our staff on _____ to begin what we hope will become an ongoing discussion about how to better support our teens and their families.

Based on *Resilience of the Soul*, a new initiative by the Department of Jewish Family Concerns of the Union for Reform Judaism, Temple _____ has begun a process of integrating resilience-building approaches into the synagogue, in the hopes of promoting health and wholeness among teens and helping them and their parents develop ways of building emotional and spiritual resilience.

All of us working together at Temple _____ consider it our ongoing responsibility to create a spiritual community in which our young people and their parents feel welcome and safe. *Resilience of the Soul* addresses this responsibility by focusing on the inner and communal resources necessary to help parents and youth meet the challenges of adolescence.

We hope the initiative will help our youth find and espouse coping methods that are safe and nurturing, so that they will avoid destructive behaviors and grow to become caring and fulfilled adults.

At this point, we would like to put together an initial task force, which we hope you will be a part of, since your perspective as a staff member and your personal experiences are invaluable. The task force will be responsible for assessing the needs of the community and gathering information, so that we can begin to plan educational sessions, including facilitated discussions with young people and their parents. We believe that through understanding the pressures as well as potential blessings that are part of this period of every Jewish life, we can gain insight into why some young people turn to harmful behaviors. We will also learn ways to foster resilience among our youth; to teach them self-nurturance and ways of coping, while making them feel cherished, loved, and cared for.

Because our families and kids have ongoing relationships with members of our staff, we expect that once we introduce this initiative, our young people and parents will turn to members of our staff to share their concerns and experiences. We want to ensure that each of us has had a chance to share our wisdom and experience with one another as part of this organized effort to help us provide further support to our parents and young people.

We look forward to learning and planning together to present this important resource to our community in a sensitive and meaningful way. You are our most important resource and your contribution is fundamental to attaining the goals of this program.

In order that the synagogue can function as a safe space for teens and their families, it must function as a safe space for you. With this in mind, we feel strongly that all your needs, feelings, concerns, suggestions, opinions, and contributions should be heard. Do not hesitate to contact _____ to share any comments, suggestions, and reactions you might have.

We look forward to seeing you at our initial meeting on _____.

Sample *D'var Torah* to Introduce the Program

Several years ago Rabbi Richard Address was approached by a number of Reform Jewish professionals who were deeply concerned about the evidence of emotional distress among teenagers with whom they interacted in their congregations, youth groups, and summer camps. Over the course of several years, the staff of the Department of Jewish Family Concerns of the Union for Reform Judaism worked to learn about the lives, stresses, behaviors, and emotions of adolescents in order to formulate ways of responding that would be helpful, that would weave together the wisdom of Jewish text and tradition, the sense of community available in our congregations and camps, and the insights and information derived from the mental health and medical fields.

Early on we learned a great deal about the prevalence of sometimes alarming behaviors that signified the presence of emotional and spiritual pain—such as eating disorders, substance abuse, self-inflicted violence, and extreme risk taking. But still wondering if perhaps the level of concern evoked by the disturbing nature of these behaviors was causing confusion about the prevalence of these behaviors and stresses among young people, we set out to get more information. We organized think tanks, visits to congregations and camps, and focus groups at URJ national conferences; we spoke to clergy, lay leaders, youth advisors, camp counselors, teen campers, NFTY and Kesher members, pediatricians, teachers, psychotherapists, and specialists in trauma and recovery.

We discovered several important truths. Many kids, including those who were not involved in harmful behaviors, reported themselves as having a great deal of stress and pressure that they would like to know how to manage better. The dangerous behaviors were indeed prevalent and increasing; almost every youngster knew kids who were involved in these behaviors. These behaviors seemed to be an attempt to cope with pressures, emotions, or traumatic experiences that the young person could not effectively manage in another more constructive and wholesome way. It became clear that helping young people and their parents to discover ways of managing emotions and life stresses in more wholesome and life affirming ways would be useful to everyone, whether or not they were ever likely to become involved in more extreme behaviors. Certain life experiences were more likely to equip a person to be able to face the stresses and tough times in life—and Jewish tradition and Jewish community could make a big difference in helping to foster those life experiences.

We learned that people facing tough and challenging times need ways to find calm; they need to have spiritual and human sources of help and guidance that help them to live with a feeling of well-being, competence, and confidence. For most of us, teens and parents alike, adolescence is a tough and challenging time and our congregations are just the right place for our families to tap into the wisdom of our tradition and the power of community to foster just the kind of strengths needed to cope with tough times.

What do we know about what enables people to face tough times and to help themselves and others? What is there to learn from the narratives of the Torah?

The story of God hearing the cry of the suffering Israelite slaves and choosing Moses to confront Pharaoh and to lead the Israelites from Egypt, through the wilderness, toward the Promised Land is one that has inspired hope throughout the ages. It is about a journey from despair to hope. It is also the story about how one man came to a position of leadership; how he managed his own frustrations and fears and those of his followers; and how he came to know and feel God's will and presence in his own life and to share that awareness and understanding with all who came after him. What can we learn from studying Moses's life that can help all of us to provide what is needed for one another in our families? Our friendships? Our Jewish communities?

Moses's life began in danger and insecurity. An edict had been issued condemning Jewish male babies to death, and yet we know that he was a much-treasured child whose parents defied this order and kept him hidden. They placed him in a waterproof basket and set the basket in the water, allowing their baby to float right into the arms of the daughter of the very Pharaoh who had ordered the death of Jewish infants. Moses's sister hid in the grasses along the riverbank to see what would happen to him and to provide an encouraging explanation. His mother stayed close by, ready to offer to nurse and serve as the baby's caretaker when Pharaoh's daughter decided to adopt him. Moses's family had enough belief in the reality of destructiveness in the world to have hidden him, but they also had enough belief in the potential for goodness and rescue to have conceived of the idea of setting him and all their hopes upon the water, hoping he would be drawn out rather than drowned.

Moses was cherished and surrounded by people who modeled hope, faith, and resourcefulness even in the midst of troubled times. They chose action, believing that even when little choice appears available, we sometimes discover hidden capacities to affect our own fate.

Fortunately, few of our children are born into such ominous circumstances. Clearly, though, most parents feel as much desire as Moses's relatives to keep their children safe while wanting to set them upon positive life courses—life courses that will build their sense of hope and that will ensure opportunities for success as well as teach them invaluable lessons of survival. When we consider the worries about terrorism in our time and the fears that our children might not be afforded all of the opportunities we wish for them, we can look to this model and try to determine how we might convey that even in the most difficult of circumstances, or even in circumstances with ordinary painful challenges, it is possible to communicate a sense of optimism and trust, and to pass on to our children the unshakable knowledge that they are cherished. We can use this sacred story to consider how we can be certain our congregations are helping our young people and families to feel that they are cherished and that there are reasons to hope and to reach out even when we have fear that others might wish us harm.

Moses spent the first three years of his life with his parents and siblings. Having been returned to the family that thought he might perish and then identified as the adopted Prince of Egypt, his cries and needs were surely heard and responded to promptly and compassionately. When he grew older, Moses was returned to the Pharaoh's daughter and raised as royalty, all the while his fellow Israelites were burdened with slavery. The Torah text tells us that God did indeed hear the cries of the Israelites, even as Pharaoh's daughter had heard the cries of the infant Moses in the basket, even as his parents had responded to his cries and needs. Later, when Moses saw the burning bush and turned to observe it, it is actually *he* who responded to *God's* call; Moses was the one who stops long enough to hear God. Moses listened to what God wanted of him. God wanted him to go and confront Pharaoh, to demand freedom for the Israelites. And God listened and validated Moses's concerns. Moses was intimidated; he feared confronting Pharaoh, and he expected no one to listen to him. Moses worried about his own speech impediment; he feared that he would be a poor spokesperson. How do we know that God listened empathically to Moses and that Moses felt heard and understood? The evidence is the fact that God did not dismiss Moses's concerns about his speech. Rather, God told Moses that Moses's brother, Aaron, would accompany him and would speak in his stead. God validated Moses's concern while giving him evidence that he had the capacity to fulfill God's mission even if his speech was imperfect. Most importantly, the Hebrew verbs used convey to us that God so understood Moses's fear and hesitation that God made certain Moses would know that God would accompany him.

The text says, "And the Lord said to Moses, '*Come* to Pharaoh . . ." [italics not in original]. Rav Menachem Mendel of Kotzk[1] notes that God does not say *lekh*—go—to Pharaoh, but *bo*—come. . . . Therefore God told Moses, "come," or in other words, "Come with Me, for I will be with you wherever you are." Thus Moses came to learn that his concerns were taken seriously and that he—and we—need not confront our fears alone, because God will hear us and always be with us. Repeatedly Moses was reminded that he has managed in the past. Even his very early rescue could be called upon as a source of hope. His family and God have been with him in the past and in the future and will always be.

To feel empowered and valued, people need to have their feelings heard and validated. *Validated* does not mean "agreed with," it means understood. God does not agree with the Israelite slaves that their plight is hopeless, nor does God agree with Moses that he cannot confront Pharaoh. God hears that without help the Israelites and Moses feel incapable and God offers the help to shift their view of the situation. The Israelites cannot even imagine freedom until they come to understand that God and Moses understand their suffering and fear. Moses could not even imagine accomplishing the task of confronting Pharaoh until he knew his brother and God would be with him.

To manage tough times, to confront the Pharaohs in our own lives, each of us needs to be able to remember times when we have been helped, when our resources have been enough. Each of us needs to feel our concerns are heard, our feelings understood, that help is offered, and that we will not need to face our fears or challenges alone. Our congregations can be places where families learn to validate one another's concerns, to encourage one another, and to remain enduring sources of accompaniment and support to one another. Our congregations can offer validation, encouragement, and spiritual and practical accompaniment to our members. Our synagogues can also offer ongoing reminders of God, who is inviting us to "Come to God," and of God as an ongoing accompanying Presence in our lives.

Important as it is to feel cherished, to have our concerns heard and validated, to be offered encouragement and accompaniment, Moses, like all of us, needed to have specific skills to manage difficult situations. He needed to learn new ways to be a leader and new

---

[1] From *Iturei Torah, Parashat Bo,* p. 70.

ways to help his followers conduct themselves. When he is overwhelmed with the responsibility for this unruly band of former slaves, his father-in-law, Jethro, hears and validates his concerns that offering constant instruction and judging every dispute is too much for him. Jethro suggests that Moses appoint elders to help him. God offers the commandments, the whole Torah as a way of guiding the people, as a substitute for Moses needing to convey God's will and expectation. God offers instructions of worship and for living together that will help the people to deal with their disagreements, their feelings of guilt and anger, their desires, their gratitude, and their need for protection and a sense of safety. Moses and the Israelites needed specific tactics, skills, and guidelines to help to manage what would otherwise be overwhelming pressures and demands.

We can learn from Moses, from the story of the Exodus, and from the provision of the Torah what we need to move from feelings of confusion, enslavement, fear and despair to hopefulness, confidence, and competence. We can discover that Jewish texts offer us insight into what we need in order to cope with life's challenges, and that our synagogue communities offer us places to discuss how to apply principles that will strengthen us and our families. Our synagogue communities can also become even better at helping people to feel cherished, to have their feelings named, heard, and validated. Our synagogue communities can aide individuals in remembering ways they coped in the past and to learn new ways of managing life's challenges. Most importantly, our synagogue communities can offer ongoing opportunities to draw upon enduring human and spiritual sources of affirmation, cooperation, acceptance, and hope as they work to truly fulfill the mission of being sanctuaries, places of safety and transformation.

Developing Resilience to the Pressures and Challenges of Adolescence

What Is Resilience?

Some Basic Information

What is resilience and why would we want our kids to have it?

All of us who work with children and teens hope for lives filled with love, health, success, and happiness for them. We wish we could protect them from disappointments, from rejections, from illness, and from crushing losses. Yet perhaps what is most realistic and most precious is to give our children the strength and resilience to find fulfillment and to sustain hope in a world in which there *are* many unforeseen obstacles, as well as countless entrances to fulfillment, to joy, and to an appreciation of the holy.

Realistically, although each of us is likely to face times that are challenging, times that strain our capacities to cope, and times that are downright traumatic, some people seem to be better able to maintain their resilience, to live with a sense of hopefulness and optimism. This does not mean that they are never discouraged or hurt; no one can avoid being affected by loss; failure; rejection; ill health; or personal, natural, or national catastrophe. The concept of resiliency simply means that there *are* people who can more easily bounce back. Confronted with difficulties and setbacks, these people can more quickly recover their sense of self-worth, their sense that the world can be trusted and that they have a secure place and purpose in it. Would not it be wonderful to imagine equipping our children and ourselves to become people with these capacities for emerging from difficulties with a positive orientation toward life and living? That is exactly what resilience is—the ability to manage life's challenges in ways that promote health and wholeness, to bounce back from stresses and adversity, and to do so using means that are life affirming.

How is resilience acquired? Can congregations play a role?

Some research suggests that there are individuals who are born with greater resilience than others; but happily, research also suggests that resiliency can be taught. In fact, one of the central functions of spiritual life and community is to help to shape human experience in such a way that hope and faith are supported. We have learned that a major factor contributing to resilience is being part of a network of relationships that allows us to feel cherished and to have a sense that what happens to us matters to others.

Through the work of the Department of Jewish Family Concerns, Rabbi Richard Address has sought to stress theology of relationships—the belief that we come to know that which is holy and divine through the loving, supportive, inspiring, and ethical relationships that we develop in our congregations. Each program developed by the Department aims to help each synagogue community to become a family for its members as well as to help its member families to become more secure and supportive. In other words, we aim to make our synagogues true sanctuaries.

Are our young people really feeling stressed? Is not stress an inevitable part of life? Can anything really be done to help young people to become more resilient?

In this very tradition of relationships that inspire and help, as we have responded to concerns about the stresses and struggles of our teens and their families, we were fortunate to learn from colleagues in Israel at the Herzog Hospital Psychotrauma Center. These mental health professionals have been working to bring education and relief to those who have experienced the trauma of warfare and terrorism. It is interesting that their work has its echoes in the work of North American mental health and religious professionals who seek to offer strength and healing to those who confront the seemingly "ordinary" traumas of childhood and adolescence in contemporary culture. What have we learned from these professionals and from our own Department's experience meeting with hundreds of young people and parents around North America?

We have learned from young people; their families; and the professionals who work with them in synagogues, summer camps, and youth groups that:

- Our young people and their parents often feel enormously stressed by the cultural expectation that each young person (and adult!) should reach toward an unattainable perfection in terms of appearance, academic, athletic, and even professional achievement.
- They often feel pressured, overwhelmed, and worried about failing to live up to these academic, athletic, and social standards.
- They desperately seek acceptance and harmony in their relationships with their parents and peers, but often feel at sea about how to find this peace with others and within themselves.
- They are very interested in learning ways to achieve calm and moderation and they would wish to feel less at the mercy of cultural and emotional pressures.

We have learned that building spiritual and emotional resiliency and acquiring real tools to manage life's challenges are of interest to kids and parents. We have learned that they are interested in having their congregations, camps, and communities offer less competitive and more accepting environments in which they can learn skills that will help them to feel less pressured and more competent to manage the situations they face in their daily lives.

What are the factors that lead to greater emotional and spiritual resiliency?

We have learned that *resilience* is the ability to manage life's challenges in ways that promote health and wholeness. It is built when individuals have an opportunity to:

- Experience themselves as worthwhile, cherished, and capable.
- Share their experiences, express their concerns, and have their feelings validated.
- Remember positive ways in which they have managed in the past.
- Discover new ways to solve problems and find calm.
- Draw upon human and spiritual sources of affirmation, cooperation, acceptance, and hope.

We have learned that whether a young person is struggling with the experience of being rejected by his or her former best friends or with hearing of tragedies affecting the physical survival of neighbors, certain factors influence his or her ability to manage the feelings in such a way that hopefulness triumphs over hurt and discouragement.

We don't mean to trivialize the suffering caused by warfare or the death of a family member by suggesting that some of the factors that assist in coping with such events also help the girl who fears being rejected by the college she hopes to attend or the boy whose first girlfriend has just told him she is breaking up with him. We are simply suggesting two truths: (1) The strengths that help us to get through the toughest of times also are of great use to us with smaller strains and challenges. (2) What appear to be minor slights and disappointments to us can have a devastating impact upon a moody, impulsive youngster. Youngsters need the tools to manage now, despite the fact that maturity will eventually bring a more nuanced point of view.

Using this model of resilience, let's look at how this might be helpful to a parent or a young person facing a specific situation so that we move from the theoretical to the practical. This will help us to understand how we might use this approach in all of our synagogue programming.

How do we help people to experience themselves as worthwhile, cherished, and capable? How will this help them to better manage emotions and stresses?

This is about how essential it is for each of us to feel we matter, that we are cherished, and that the world needs us here. We can get through a lot if we have grown up with such a sense of our own value; life will be a continual struggle against despair if we do not. Religion can help a lot here! Religious faith can help us to feel that we exist for a reason, that we are loved and needed by the Creator, and that we have a contribution to make to the fulfillment of the divine plan. Each of us needs to feel specifically cherished, and usually it is easier to believe that we are treasured by God if we have experienced unconditional human love. We start out as parents, spouses, friends, or synagogue professionals believing that this is a central goal that we have for ourselves, and we hope and expect that our spouses, children, friends, and congregants will feel valued and cherished.

Yet there is a big difference between our intent and even our actions and gestures and what the individual actually may receive and perceive. When someone has experienced something that shakes his or her confidence and feeling of being valued, something extra is required to restore this. This is true, for instance, if the person has had open-heart surgery and countless hours have been spent to save his or her life. Certain factors will determine whether the experience results in feeling valued and cherished, or reduced and disregarded. If he or she is treated with respect and gentleness, called by name by the hospital staff, afforded contact with family, and spoken to rather than about, chances are a sense of being cherished will prevail. If he or she is treated as the patient in bed 7 in the coronary intensive care unit, as a heart to be monitored rather than as a whole person, as a tangle of tubes and symptoms, with body attended to but spirit ignored, then depression and despair are much more likely to set in. This is also true if the person in question is a twelve-year-old girl who has not been invited to bar and bat mitzvah parties of friends with whom she has been close since she was three; or if the person in question is a seventeen-year-old boy who has just been rejected from his first-choice college; or if the person in question is a fifty-year-old man or woman whose marriage has just ended. In each of these situations, the person faces a crisis that shakes his or her sense of being someone loved and valued. Having bad things happen to us can make us feel that we are worthless.

In the case of terrorism and warfare, it is obvious. When people are shooting at you, you don't feel cherished and valued. Even in extreme situations, however, it is possible to develop resilience through feeling cherished. In his work, Dr. Victor Frankl, a survivor of Theresienstadt and Auschwitz concentration camps, examined which people fared best spiritually and emotionally in Holocaust concentration camps. He discovered that even when they were mistreated, those who fared the best spiritually and emotionally were those that felt cherished by someone and could cherish others, even if only in their memories. Individuals who could remember being cherished by loved ones and could hold onto those memories and hope for reunion, and those who could behave in a way that made them feel they were still civilized and caring, were able to maintain better emotional, spiritual, and even physical health.

When people have been victims of terrible acts of violence directed against them by others or by natural disasters, offering loving gestures that show that they are not forgotten by the world is a way of restoring a sense of worth and trust. Speaking to someone by name; remembering that person's name; connecting him or her with loved ones, either literally or by conversing with them about loved ones; and asking questions that allow the person to speak of his or her own sense of competency that was shattered by the recent event all restore to the person the sense that he or she is neither a number nor a forgotten victim, but a person who has a role, who has belonged, and who has had and will have love.

Parents will naturally wonder how it could be that a child they showered with love could doubt being cherished. Yet when parents are asked to bring to mind their recent interactions with their actual teens, their recollection will often not be of a loving exchange; they may remember having conveyed a sense that their child's behavior was a source of parental stress. Sure, they still love their teen, but many teens will report that they think their parents liked them better when they were younger or that their parents disapprove of how they look, how they act, or how they speak. In fact, the teen may be equally or more disapproving of his or her parents.

Yet it is in this very atmosphere that teenagers need to be reminded somehow of their worth and that they are cherished for who they are. They need to know that they bring inestimable joy and meaning to their parents' lives. Sharing this message and having it come across are not easy.

Each teen needs to feel a sense of capability and competence. Not every teen is an athlete, a scholar, or a future fashion model. Families and communities need to focus on those areas of competence, even those not applauded by the general culture, that are potential sources of feelings of capability. The young person's specific gifts must be stressed, whether it is his or her ability to play the guitar, to be kind to his or her grandmother, to amuse his or her baby cousin, to drive safely, or to keep trying after repeated failures. Sometimes we will be called upon to help our young people to feel cherished and treasured when the trauma they are facing is one they seem to have brought upon themselves or even upon us—such as a school failure, a run-in with authorities, a violation of family rules, or being kicked off a team.

Do parents need to develop resiliency too?
Can the congregation help?

Paradoxically, parents themselves often do not feel very cherished or capable. Their children often behave in dismissive ways and parents do not necessarily feel that they are succeeding at parenting. We who seek to guide parents often fill them with alarm about all of the bad effects of poor parenting when what parents need to be reminded of is that when teens list what they worry about most, it is usually "disappointing their parents." What they crave most is to be able to talk openly and be understood by their parents, the very parents about whose opinion they claim not to care at all.

Parents need to be reminded that their kids love them very much even if they cannot express it right now. Parents also need help to take a break from focusing their attention on their kids and provide a sense of being cherished by one another. They need their congregations to make them feel that they are cherished members, not just because they are needed to make a minyan or to volunteer at the bake sale or in the parking lot during religious school, but because they are a treasured part of the congregational family. How is this conveyed? By learning names, seeking to have ways in which synagogue staff comes to know families and individuals one by one, and seeking ways that members come to personally know and care about one another.

The statistics bear this out. The greater the degree to which individuals feel that they are known and cherished by their families, their friends, their faith communities, and their colleagues, the more they are able to bounce back and bear life's stresses. Simple membership in a family, congregation, or social group affords no protection if it is an anonymous or indifferent or hostile connection. There are things that each congregation and each family and each individual can do to help to build such ties. And Judaism encourages ties of love, fidelity, and mutual care among couples, between parents and children, among congregants, among Jews, and between Jews and their neighbors.

Why does it help when people have an opportunity to share their experiences, express their concerns, and have their feelings validated?

Most of us are used to hearing that when there has been a disaster like a devastating tornado or fire, or an act of terrorism, that along with other aid provided, counselors are brought in to listen to the accounts of those who have been affected. It might seem like the counseling could wait until later—and we might expect that the counseling is about where to find housing, health care, or financial assistance, not emotional support. In fact, one of the most important ways of helping people who have been through a difficult time is to simply allow and encourage them to tell their story—to relate to how they feel about what has occurred and to validate their feelings. When people have experienced something unsettling and disturbing, they may need to tell their story over and over, only gradually being able to name and express their own feelings. They may need to be told over and over that their feelings are understandable. This is true when a woman has gone through a difficult labor and delivery. This is true when a person has survived a car accident. This is true when a teenager has failed a road test. This is true when an eleven-year-old has witnessed a violent crime. This is true when a woman has been physically assaulted. This is true when an individual has lost a job.

We don't need to be professional counselors to provide this for one another. Often we don't know exactly what we are feeling, and it is helpful to have the time to sort it out. It is even comforting to have the other person give a name to what we are feeling (e.g., "Were you angry? Scared? Disappointed?"). Listening to people is a way of letting them know that they and their feelings are important.

What is the difference between validating feelings and agreeing with them?

What exactly is meant by validating feelings? It isn't as natural and easy as it sounds, but it is very helpful. It means acknowledging what the other person feels and not trying to talk him or her out of it, even when our intention is positive.

When a person has lost his job and says, "My life is ruined. My family cannot survive. I am a total failure," we want to respond, "It isn't ruined! Your family will survive. After all, your wife has a job, too. You are certainly not a failure, think of all your successes. You will get another job." There *is* a time to say those things, a time when they will be helpful. First, we need to communicate that what the person is feeling is valid, that we hear it, that we understand it, that we can even imagine how painful the feeling is. A validating response might be, "You are feeling so devastated and discouraged, I can hear you think things will never get better and that you are so worried about your family. Losing your job has just made you feel like a total failure. How painful to feel that way." A validating response does not mean that we're agreeing with the person. It *does* mean that we communicate respect for them and acknowledge that their feelings and opinions are legitimate.

Another nonvalidating response would be, "Stop feeling so sorry for yourself! You are not the first person to lose a job, and didn't you show up late a lot? For goodness sake, you aren't a failure. You made twice what I do! Talk about failure, I am a failure!" In this case, the person is told not to feel what he or she feels, is made to look at how he or she might have contributed to the situation, and is asked to consider how much worse someone else's situation is. Although speaking unkindly is rarely helpful, considering how one's own actions may have contributed to the situation, considering one's own situation compared to others, and moving beyond self-pity might be useful. Initially, however, when we have been hurt or disappointed, we need to feel that we have a right to our feelings and that others support and accept our emotions.

How can you validate the feelings and opinions of a teen who is saying what seems to us to be preposterous things?

With teens, validating their feelings might mean validating the young person's perception, even if that means agreeing that nothing is his or her fault or that he or she is given too little freedom. He or she may say, "It wasn't my fault! I came home late because you didn't let me go out until after all of my work was done. You didn't give me enough time with my friends. The curfew was unfair!" Most of us would want to respond, "That is just an excuse. You could have done your work earlier, you just don't want to comply with my rules. You are grounded!" There is time to figure out how we want to respond to the curfew infraction, but we can still say, "You don't want to be blamed. It doesn't feel like it is your fault. You felt you didn't have enough time with your friends. You felt I was unfair."

Even when teens are expressing feelings or ideas that don't anger us, we may tend to be invalidating because we wish they didn't feel emotional pain. When a youngster says, "I wasn't invited because I am ugly and unpopular! I am such a geek! Look at my hair! I will never have a boyfriend/girlfriend. Nothing goes right for me," we want to rush in with reassurance. We want to say, "You are so pretty, and you were invited to so many other parties. Your hair looks fine to me. I felt just as you do and I found someone. Last week you were accepted to the program you wanted to get into. Lots of things go right for you." The validating response, however, would be one that acknowledges that the young person is hurt at not being invited; that he or she worries about being unattractive and fears ending up alone and rejected.

Why is this so important? It is important because our feelings are less overwhelming if we do not experience them alone. It is also important because we cannot begin to find solutions before we really understand what we feel. We are more likely to come to reflect upon the fact that sometimes our feelings don't correspond to the reality when we hear them reflected back to us without ridicule or rebuttal.

Why is it important to help people remember positive ways in which they have managed in the past?

When we have a reservoir of personal successes upon which to draw, when we hit adversity we are more able to believe we will get through the challenge. Two things are necessary here: to have had positive coping experiences and to be able to remember them.

In working with teens and parents, it is important to offer opportunities to have experiences of success and to help them to view past experiences in a positive light. The successes and positive ways of managing do not need to have been winning prizes or juggling three jobs. The person who has experienced a loss can be reminded—after he or she is made to feel valued and his or her feelings have been validated—that he or she felt this way when, for instance, a grandparent died years ago. That was painful and yet, in time, he or she felt better and was able to go on, comforted by good memories.

When a parent who cannot get her preteen to study for his bar mitzvah shares her worries with us, we can confirm her feelings by agreeing that it is a tough and frustrating process. We can validate her fear that her child will get up on the bimah and not be able to read the Torah. We can also, however, remind her that she trained her son to use a toilet; he didn't go to kindergarten in diapers, even though she once felt he would never use the potty. We can tell her that she has a good track record at managing difficult situations with her somewhat stubborn son.

The high school student who is certain he cannot master calculus can be reminded that he didn't think he could learn his multiplication tables either. The student can be helped to remember how he coped with learning those math facts. The mother, who wants to help, can be reminded to think of how she toilet trained her son. Both mother and child can draw upon their own past positive experiences.

The basic message is that the present situation is tough, but you have got what it takes because you have gotten through some tough things in the past. Small successes are as important as major triumphs, because usually we need to take small steps to begin to transcend the difficulties facing us now.

How can congregations urge people toward change while supporting their past means of coping?

It is very important for congregations to integrate this approach in educational work with parents, teens, and staff since it is a common practice to try to motivate people to become involved in programs about life-cycle events by raising anxiety—anxiety about situations they will face in the future, in the hopes that they will then want to participate.

For instance, often we try to engage parents by urging them to come in for family programs so that they will be prepared for all of the stresses associated with *b'nei mitzvah* preparation. We offer examples of what can go wrong if they are not on top of things and we may even urge them in good faith to come to learn about the very negative behavior that sometimes occurs at *b'nei mitzvah* parties. This is information we want people to have, but we may inadvertently raise everyone's anxiety about an already stressful event. What we want to do instead is give them facts and strategies to have things proceed in a wholesome way, consistent with the parents' and congregation's values.

It is a challenge to stress the positive. For example, we might advertise that workshops will be offered to help families to create celebrations that will reflect the values that they have been emphasizing in raising their children all along. The title might be, "It's YOUR Family's Celebration: Making Your Celebration Personal, Positive, and Memorable." This is much more positive than a workshop entitled: "Do You Know What Your Kids Are Doing on the Bus? The Perils of the Early Teen Years." The same thing applies to sessions about college admission, cancer prevention, and Jewish continuity. Are we raising anxiety and causing people to panic, or are we offering programs that will help them to feel that the congregation is a place to find calm and encouragement—a place that will help them have faith that they can and will cope with the situations that life presents?

Is it really possible to discover new ways to solve problems and find calm? What can the congregation offer in this regard? Does our tradition offer routes to greater inner peace?

We want parents and teens to remember that they have coped in the past. We do not want to simply generate a great deal of anxiety, but we want to acknowledge that they may be facing some serious challenges now, and that there may be more ahead.

Far too few congregants, whether they are adults or kids, consider their synagogue to be a place where they can seek assistance in managing life's stresses. They believe that the synagogue offers ethical guidance, and they know that friendships they have made at the synagogue may be a source of support, but still they do not turn to the synagogue for practical help. Central to the function of religious life, however, is the belief that the religious community must inspire and support faith and hope; the notion that we and the world around us have what we need to prevail amidst ordinary and sometimes extraordinary stresses. The ability to hold onto optimism and remain calm makes it easier to strategize, to find solutions, and to recover some sense of peace in the midst of difficulty. This notion is central to the idea of resiliency.

Our traditional texts and Jewish history provide models for dealing with complex and challenging situations. Our liturgy and poetry provide opportunities for reflection, for reaching out for comfort and strength, and for giving voice to our deepest feelings. In this spirit, our congregations can and should become places where young people and adults can discover new avenues for self-expression and self-soothing, and for maintaining physical, spiritual, and emotional well-being. In this way, the synagogue becomes a place where people reach for health, for wholeness, and for holiness.

Are there specific programs that the congregation can offer that promote healthy ways of reducing stress?

In order for teenagers (and their parents) to manage stress, they need to be getting enough rest, eating nutritiously, and exercising at a healthy level. We can provide information that will encourage these positive behaviors and habits.

Judaism has always stressed that the soul, mind, and body are connected and that spiritual well-being is intricately connected to the way we care for our bodies. The great Jewish scholar Maimonides was also a physician whose work remains a central spiritual guide. He stressed moderation and self-care. Synagogues can offer programs on nutrition in which members can evaluate how they are eating, can learn ways to eat that will sustain health, and can learn Jewish teachings on how what we eat can add to our sense of holiness. Programs can be offered right in the synagogue that give young people the opportunity for exercise that reduces stress, strengthens the body, and also increases confidence.

Some synagogues have offered programs in noncompetitive sports; others have created wilderness programs modeled on Israeli scouting programs, offering a Judaic "spin" on activities that promote wellness. Many members of the clergy have developed an expertise in Jewish meditation practices that can be integrated in services or offered as classes for adults and teens. The congregation can offer Jewish journaling, an opportunity to find calm and self expression through facilitated workshops on keeping journals and writing poetry and song lyrics. Students could look to the Jewish tradition for inspiration, such as King David who poured out his doubts and fears in psalms, and Anne Frank whose spirit was sustained through the recording of the complex and rich emotions she experienced when in hiding during the Holocaust. Examples of some of these programs and of how some congregations have introduced them will be offered in this guide (see "Keeping a Creative Journal" on page 143).

Aren't we speaking about emotional as well as spiritual health? Should mental health professionals be involved? Aren't these issues better handled in school health classes and therapists' offices?

Conceiving of the synagogue as a place to make connections and to facilitate healthy living and self expression, we can invite health professionals to join with clergy and Jewish educators. These specialists can present new ways of understanding adolescent development, conflict resolution, family relationships, and skills that help with regulating emotion. The congregation need not seek to become a clinical or therapeutic milieu; rather, it ought to serve as a sanctuary where members bring their deepest concerns and develop wholesome and spiritually sound ways of managing life. In those situations that require clinical intervention, nonetheless, the congregation can offer appropriate referrals while providing ongoing support and encouragement. (Please consult the following chapter in this section, "Coping in Ways That Hurt Us" (page 27) for guidance on preventing and responding to such situations.)

What does it mean to teach people to "draw upon human and spiritual sources of affirmation, cooperation, acceptance, and hope"? How can we help people to find those resources within Jewish life?

There are many programs that can be offered that teach members of synagogues how they might better manage stress and that link them to Jewish teachings and rituals that can prove healing and inspiring. It is the way that the synagogue functions as a community, however, that has the most promise in promoting resilience. Belonging to a community that values us, knowing that our presence matters, and knowing that the details of our lives are of interest to those who share our community are important sources of affirmation for every one of us. Yet all too many people who belong to synagogues do not reap this benefit; they may feel alone and discouraged even in a full sanctuary.

It is easy to dismiss the complaints of those who feel alone and ill at ease in the synagogue by suggesting that if they came more often and involved themselves on committees, the synagogue would become a second home to them. For our congregations to become places that promote resilience, we need to work toward viewing each person who enters the synagogue as someone who may have experienced a trauma or difficult stress and is in need of our help and the help of our tradition to reach toward hope. If we approached each person—child, teen, and adult—with this vision of what we can be for one another, we would create an atmosphere to which people would be drawn as they traverse the difficult paths that are part of every life. We can work to be certain that the way the staff and lay leaders communicate with one another is validating. Even when we cannot agree to what others may want of us, we can convey a sense of confidence that solutions to problems can be found. This may mean validating a congregant's desire to always find a convenient parking space or to have his or her child learn Hebrew without attending regularly. We can communicate acceptance of what people feel even as we may not be able to provide exactly what they wish we could.

In fact, the validation most people are really looking for is not for what is impossible. It is usually simply to hear mention made and consideration given to those issues that are central to their lives. They want to hear that there is a place in the sanctuary, the classroom, and the meeting room for their concerns. They want a place to voice their and their children's fears of failure and to express the pressures for financial, academic, and personal achievement that exist alongside battles with illness, addiction, depression, and loneliness. They want to know there is a place for all the complex emotions that are part of their lives. They want to know that by coming to synagogue and by being part of this community they and their children will gain wisdom, skills, and faith to be better able to manage life. They truly want their Jewish faith and their Jewish learning to help them to become more resilient, and it can.

Coping in Ways That Hurt Us

Information about Self-Destructive Behaviors

Why are some people more likely to engage in self-destructive behaviors?

Much of this guide is devoted to promoting emotional and spiritual resilience through encouraging the development of positive and adaptive ways of coping with stress. It is nonetheless important to acknowledge that all of us will have moments when we simply feel overwhelmed. How often these occur, how much stress it takes to trigger that kind of response, and how extreme and long lasting our distress will be, depends on many factors.

Some of us are clearly born with a lower threshold for coping with stress. We respond more to less stimulation. We somehow seem to feel everything more acutely than others for whom it takes much more to ruffle their feathers. Some of us have had a great deal of over–whelming stress early in life, either because of illness, parental problems, extreme poverty, or warfare. We have had to cope with too much too soon and are left more vulnerable.

Regardless of the reason, all of us can be helped to find safe and healthy ways to return to a state of greater calm. Along the way, however, some of us get involved in seeking to reduce our distress in ways that are potentially harmful.

How can something that hurts us help us to feel better?

It may seem like a paradox, the notion that we might do something that actually hurts us in our efforts to feel better. Yet if we stop to think about it, every one of us has engaged in some action meant to offer temporary relief that in the long run probably was more likely to do some damage, however mild.

Material for this chapter has been derived from a number of sources including chapters in books by Dr. Shelley Doctors, and Tracy Alderman, *The Scarred Soul: Understanding and Ending Self-Inflicted Violence* (Oakland, CA: New Harbinger Publications, 1997).

Which of us has not reached for, and even polished off, a whole box of cookies after we were involved in a distressing conversation? Perhaps we get angry at a spouse or a relative and soothe ourselves with the sweet and crunchy snack, feeling a sense of pleasure and well-being come over us as the hurtful words recede into the back of our minds? Minutes later we may feel regret and even some self-loathing at our loss of control. Perhaps we're reminded of the effect of overeating when we notice the snugness of our clothing; perhaps we're recalling the words of our internist cautioning us to lose weight and avoid sugary desserts. In any case, now we feel bad both about the conversation *and* about the cookies; and yet, at that moment of temporary distress, eating those cookies certainly provided us some brief comfort and distraction. We have not resolved the original problem by eating the cookies. We are also likely to reach for cookies when we are upset the next time, even though we suffered pangs of regret and felt like the overeating was a bad choice. Sure, it wasn't good for us, but it tasted good.

Food can have effects on the brain that make us feel better. We felt bad; we found something that at least temporarily felt good and odds are we're going to do it again. This is a "normal," everyday example of a bit of self-destructive behavior that offers soothing. Although minor in degree, it has many of the same features as other more serious self-harming behaviors, such as drinking alcohol. Perhaps if we can remember that "ordinary" folks engage in drinking too much, shopping too much, gambling, smoking, or doing other activities to distract and soothe themselves from problems—even though these solutions worsen their situation in the long run—we will be better able to empathize with them and understand the more serious self-harming behaviors.

Why does this provide relief for some people and why is it dangerous?

The more serious behaviors that we refer to are the ones that some young people choose or find themselves involved with as a way of trying to cope with or escape difficult feelings. They include self-mutilating behaviors like superficial cutting or burning of the skin (not in order to commit suicide or cause major injury), binge drinking and eating, self-starvation, and extreme risk taking.

Just as the person who reaches for the cookies is seeking to get relief from tension, anger, and disappointment, the young person who engages in more seriously self-destructive or self-injuring behavior is seeking to get relief from intense and unsettling emotions.

Food tastes good so it is easier to understand that choice. Scientists and clinicians note that gambling and other risk-taking behavior may produce thrills, a sense of excitement, and even temporary feelings of invulnerability. Just as food can be used healthfully to satisfy nutritional needs while providing pleasure through taste and even positive associations, other normal avenues for meeting physical and emotional needs can be used compulsively or dangerously.

While there is some disagreement in our culture about what constitutes healthy and appropriate sexual behavior, particularly among young people, most of us see masturbation as a natural expression of sexuality during the teenage years. Yet masturbation can become a compulsive way of discharging tensions that has little to do with sexual pleasure and much to do with anxieties that are only temporarily eased in this manner. Some young people express their desire for escapist thrill-seeking through driving fast and taking unnecessary risks; others engage in the "choking game," in which a high is produced as oxygen supply is meant to be temporarily cut off through tightening something around the neck. Sometimes young people use some means of choking themselves while masturbating, because they have been told there will be added pleasure. While noncompulsive masturbation is seen by most liberal Jews as a normal means of sexual discharge, when it is accompanied by an attempt at partial asphyxia, it can prove deadly. Many teens have lost their lives experimenting with these dangerous choking games. Such activities are attempts at finding pleasure or distraction in the face of emotional pain that can prove quite dangerous. It is not always easy to assess when a behavior or practice has moved from the more normal or usual realm, to when it has become a compulsive attempt to gain distance from problems and feelings that need to be approached and resolved in a more healthful manner.

But what can be said of actual, direct injury to the body? Research suggests that when there is a physical trauma, even self-induced, endorphins are released that have effects similar to morphine. This means that the person will not feel the pain of the sustained injury and will, in addition, be distracted from the original emotional pain. Scientists tell us that whenever endorphins are released there is the potential for an addictive response. Dr. Tracy Alderman, an expert on self-inflicted violence, notes that, "Anything that provides a biochemical pathway to relief may be sought again creating habits that are potentially quite destructive and leave underlying problems untouched while offering temporary soothing." Dr. Alderman provides additional explanation for why such harmful behaviors may be chosen:

> Self-destructive behaviors may serve functions beyond distraction and a temporary feeling of wellbeing. Sometimes they serve as a means of communicating distress when words are unavailable or fail. Sometimes they serve as physical expressions of an internal conflict. Paradoxically, creating a physical injury or impairing ability to function may enable the young person to provide for him/herself or get from others the nurturance and caretaking that he or she could not ask for directly. Sometimes the young person is very self critical and self-hurt is a form of self-punishment. Young people who have been physically abused and traumatized sometimes replicate the past hurt so that they can feel in control. Many people involved in these behaviors cannot explain them, but know that they are emotionally uncomfortable and feel compelled to do what they do.[1]

Isn't this a problem affecting only a small number of young people? Can it really be life-threatening? Isn't it rare in the Jewish community?

Evidence provided by teens, teachers, pediatricians, parents, camp counselors, and youth workers suggests that these behaviors are far more common than anyone previously thought, and that they occur as frequently within the Jewish community as anywhere else. In fact, self-mutilating behavior either is increasing or increasingly reported. While extreme self-injury may occur with more frequency and severity among hospitalized patients struggling

---

[1]Tracy Alderman, "Why Do People Engage in Self-Inflicted Violence?" *The Prevention Researcher* 7, no.4 (November 2000): 11.

with more serious mental illness, high-functioning teens may also be secretly engaging in these behaviors as a way of coping with intense feelings.

The quest for perfection and high achievement that is endemic to many of our communities inadvertently contributes to the pressures experienced by young people. Of course not all young people who experience pressure to excel will become symptomatic or engage in self-harming behavior. Yet, those who feel unable to manage the pressure or to calm themselves in safer ways do engage in these behaviors, and they actually teach one another to find relief in these ways.

There is definitely a contagion effect; some will try these behaviors briefly and give them up; others may get hooked on this way of escaping inner distress and end up scarred and unable to stop themselves. Unfortunately, the problem is compounded because the pressures to appear fine and successful and the stigma attached to emotional problems causes many young people and their parents to hide all signs of vulnerability and need for help.

While binge drinking and binge eating are more easily understood by most of us to be ways of self-soothing that go awry, few of us initially think of anorexia, another eating disorder, as a way of managing confusing feelings and seeking calm. While we do not understand all of the physiological factors that may make one young person more likely to begin and continue to starve him- or herself, we do know that there are many cultural and emotional factors that contribute to the development of this disorder.

In the midst of the sometimes turbulent emotions that come with early adolescence, many young girls and a smaller number of young boys seem to gain a sense of control by carefully regimenting their food intake and exercise. The cultural imperatives that dictate the ideal of being slender and even skinny are felt keenly by these young people, and they believe that they will be successful and perfect only when they have attained a very low weight. For many, the limiting of food intake is accompanied by intense and relentless exercise regimes. In our contemporary atmosphere in which preoccupation with diet and fitness seem so ubiquitous, it may take some time to recognize that a young person has carried this to an extreme. Some youngsters, often boys, may not diet but may be obsessed with their body contours, abusing steroids and weight lifting in an attempt to feel powerful and perfect.

These behaviors can and sadly often do become life threatening; and like many other self-destructive behaviors, because starvation and extreme exercise can produce feelings of euphoria, they actually become addictive. At a certain point judgment is lost about actual appearance and a threat to health becomes very real. All more usual adolescent concerns get swept away as the young person thinks only of food and of controlling intake and of maximizing exercise to burn calories and change the body. In this way, all of the difficult decisions, challenges, and pressures of adolescence recede to be replaced by these dangerous preoccupations and behaviors, again not solving the original problems, but rather replacing them with new ones.[2]

It is also very important to note that while most self-harming behavior is an attempt to seek calm and a sense of reduced tension rather than to cause death, death can be the unintended outcome. The young person who binge drinks, binge eats and purges, drives cars recklessly, plays the "choking game," or cuts or burns him- or herself may actually inadvertently create a life-threatening situation.

---

[2]Please see the URJ Department of Jewish Family Concerns publication *Litapayach Tikvah*, "To Nourish Hope," for more information about a Jewish response to eating disorders.

This is also an important place to note the need to recognize and address depression in our communities because in not doing so we really leave so many young people in great peril. While most people who engage in self-harming behaviors do not end up taking their own lives, some young people who have engaged in these behaviors do go on to actually make suicide attempts if their despair and depression worsen.

Because of this, it is important to recognize the emotional pain and the lack of adequate tools with which to lessen this pain, and to provide opportunities for emotional expression and compassionate assistance in managing these feelings. By recognizing that many young people who engage in these behaviors are struggling with undiagnosed depression for which they are unknowingly attempting to treat themselves, we go a long way to removing the aura of judgment and disapproval. This does not mean that we must condone binge drinking or reckless driving or even deliberate self-injury; we must not. These behaviors are of great concern to us. Yet, it is easier to see that the young person who cuts him- or herself is in emotional pain than to consider that the young person who returns home drunk every night of the weekend after partying may not be having so much fun after all.

It is important to educate synagogue staff, parents, and young people about the signs of depression and of suicide risk in young people. Of greatest significance is recognizing that the risk is greater just because adolescence is a time when mood changes may be swift and judgment of consequences not yet fully developed; when there has not yet been much experience with transcending problems; and when there is a disinclination to admit the need for adult help.

Suicide attempts can be made impulsively by a young person who has not appeared depressed but who has had a crushing disappointment—and what is experienced as a crushing disappointment by a teen could include the end of a first romance, a public embarrassment, or any event that is a major blow to reputation or self-esteem. Even in our age of supposedly greater openness and acceptance of homosexuality, being gay or transgender vastly increases the young person's chances of making a suicide attempt, because there is a fear of disappointing parents, of being different, or of having a romance end without there being anyone in whom to confide.

Of course, few young people, gay or straight, will deal with feelings of depression, shame, or discouragement by attempting suicide. It is essential, nonetheless, that everyone knows the risk factors and danger signs and knows how to get help for themselves and for others. This is one more important reason for addressing ignorance and misunderstanding about homosexuality and gender issues in our communities since doing so will ultimately save lives.[3]

What can congregations do to help?

In order to increase the likelihood that those who are struggling will reach out for help, the most important thing we can do is to work to keep lines of communication open. In our synagogue settings we can do this by acknowledging that emotional distress ought not to be hidden or treated as something shameful. We can openly discuss our awareness that many

---

[3]For additional information please see the URJ Department of Jewish Family Concerns publication *Kulanu: All of Us*, our program guide for congregations implementing GLBTI inclusion.

young people do become involved in self-destructive behaviors. Anything that we can do to diminish isolation, denial, shame, and hopelessness will be a step toward connection and healing. Of course, once we become aware that a young person is engaging in self-harming behavior, we hope that by referring them for help the behaviors will stop. In fact, it is more helpful to convey empathy for the pain that led to these behaviors, than to focus on the behavior we might find worrisome, since many people cannot stop these destructive behaviors until they have found better ways to manage their feelings. Making certain that we know where to refer youth and their families for psychotherapy and medical help is essential. But it is creating families and Jewish communities in which vulnerabilities and emotional pain can be acknowledged together that is the first step toward beginning to find solutions.

What does Judaism have to say about self-harming behaviors?

We may wonder what Judaism has to say about engaging in self-harming behaviors. While our Jewish tradition urges us to always choose life and stresses that we have within us the capacity to take the life-affirming, positive path, it is important not to use this to further the young person's guilt. Rather, we want them to understand that choosing a life-affirming path is the goal, and that if they have strayed from such a path it is because of emotional pain that felt unmanageable. We must stress that we want that person to avail themselves of help offered not because they have violated a Jewish principle, but because an even more central principle teaches us that each of us is made in the image of God, and that means each of us is of infinite value and therefore worthy of care and protection.

Of course, it is natural to react with shock and dismay if we come upon a person engaged in an action that will cause harm. It is difficult to resist the impulse to express that sense of horror and even anger. When we are able to express concern for the underlying emotional distress, as well as optimism that relief can be found in other ways, it is then that we are more truly "walking in God's ways," responding to the cry, and helping the person take the first step toward freedom.

How can my congregation help?

We may also wonder how congregations can help. Our tradition reminds us that we need one another and that we are most likely to make healthy, ethical choices when we feel we are fully integrated members of families and communities that are sanctuaries for our souls. At the same time, aspects of our Jewish tradition and culture may inadvertently serve to encourage excessive guilt and perfectionism by encouraging us to acknowledge only the most noble of feelings. Perfectionism, then, may be the inadvertent result of our often-positive value of seeking always to try to improve ourselves, our families, and our world. Congregations can strive to help young people to see the difference between perfectionism and seeking to improve ourselves and our world. We are not expected to complete the job of repairing the world or ourselves, we are only expected to involve ourselves in the process.

We can help our congregants to consider aspects of our tradition, like those observed on Yom Kippur, which offer self-denial and self-affliction as means of achieving forgiveness and closeness to God. These may be misapplied by the person who is in despair who may decide that if self-denial is an aid to repentance on Yom Kippur, it is even more holy and helpful to fast and afflict oneself on ordinary days. It is very helpful to discuss that in fact, Jewish tradition very strictly limits fasting and self-denial to specific days and discourages vows to restrain one's eating and drinking (such as in the case of the Nazirite, a type of Jewish ascetic). Instead the focus is upon moderation and the responsibility to care for the body, which is the house of the soul. Note though, that this will only be helpful to the young person if he or she is helped to find other ways of understanding and reducing feelings of sinfulness or self-loathing.

We can model our congregational response on the Jewish belief that the greatest relief and healing can be achieved when one person's despair is recognized and helped by another. Our tradition teaches us that when King Saul was melancholy, David's presence, music of his harp, and song offered Saul solace (I Samuel 16:23); from this we can learn that companionship, prayer, and song can be powerful sources of help and transformation for the person who is suffering, and we can seek to make our congregations places where this is available to all.

While people who engage in self-inflicted violence and other self-harming behaviors need professional help, they can find support and comfort in their Jewish communities. Judaism and Jewish community can offer a sense of belonging and of hope. Our communities can become sacred places where all kinds of feelings are acknowledged—the painful experiences of envy, rage, despair, and loneliness along with the joyous experiences of companionship, celebration, accomplishment, and cooperation.

Our communities, from our early childhood programs through confirmation and beyond, can be places where together we seek within our traditions and our wisdom for better ways to manage the trials that are part of every life. Families can find understanding and respect instead of stigma and criticism even when one member or another has become overwhelmed by life. Seeking within our sacred texts, we can learn from the experiences of biblical and Talmudic figures that grappling with loss, disappointment, failure, jealousy, and hurt have been challenging also to those who came before us, and that together we can find ways of coping that are not destructive.

A few words spoken during Shabbat or festival services acknowledging the struggles teens and families may be experiencing can be a simple and profound way of letting people know that the deepest concerns of their lives are understood in the synagogue. As is stated in Proverbs 16:24, "Encouraging words are as honey, sweet to the soul and health to the being." Ancient prayers can be adapted to offer a link to contemporary concerns, thereby offering people words with which to express what is in their hearts, offering alternatives to destructive action, and giving voice to the longing for the help of God and community.

Suicide Prevention

Pikuach Nefesh, The Obligation to Save a Life

כָּל הַמְאַבֵּד נֶפֶשׁ אַחַת כְּאִילּוּ אִבֵּד עוֹלָם מָלֵא, וְכָל הַמְקַיֵּים נֶפֶשׁ אַחַת
כְּאִילּוּ קַיֵּים עוֹלָם מָלֵא.

"Whoever causes the loss of a single soul it is as if they have caused the loss of a world entire,
and whoever saves a single soul it is as if they have saved a universe."

—Talmud, *Sanhedrin* 37a

Suicide is a universal problem. There is no particular type of person who takes his or her own life. People of every race, religion, sex, and age commit suicide. In the Jewish tradition, the sanctity of life is understood from the notion that every human being was created in the image of God, thus making each person's life of inestimable value. Consequently, the obligation to prevent suicide and thus to save a life is of the highest order. That being said, in some cases suicide is not preventable, and we ought not blame ourselves for having failed to save a life. *"Lo aleicha hamlakha ligmor,"* teaches Rabbi Tarfon in the Mishnah (Pirkei Avot 2:21): "we are not obligated to complete the task, we are obligated to try."

When dealing with someone who may be at risk for suicide it is crucial that our response be more than simply expressing a sense of shock or dismay about the possibility of suicide. In other words, despite our instinct to do just that, we have to remember to convey empathy and openness to the person's pain, rather than act horrified by the mention of suicide. The point is to keep the person alive long enough to get help, which, despite our best intentions, is less likely to happen when we yell out "suicide is horrible!" Rather, a more helpful thing to say would be "you must be in so much pain to be thinking of suicide. How hard this must be for you!"

❑ *Some information on youth and suicide:*
  • Suicide is the third-leading cause of death among youth overall (ages 15–24).
  • Suicide is the second-leading cause of death among college students (male and female together).

Information in this chapter was gleaned from the Jed Foundation Website (http://www.jedfoundation.org) and the URJ-JFC Web site (http://www.urj.org/jfc/)

35

- Suicide attempts pose the *greatest* life-threatening danger for college women.
- Four out of five young adults who attempt suicide have given clear warnings.
- Gay, lesbian, bisexual, and trangender youth commit suicide three times more often than heterosexual youth.
- Young adults of ages 18–24 think about suicide more often than any other age group.

❑ *Risk factors:*
- *Mental Illness:* 90 percent of adolescent suicide victims have at least one diagnosable, active psychiatric illness at the time of death—most often depression, substance abuse, and conduct disorders. Only 15 percent of suicide victims were in treatment at the time of death.
- *Previous Attempts:* 26–33 percent of adolescent suicide victims have made a previous suicide attempt.
- *Stressors:* Suicide in youth often occurs after the victim has gotten into trouble or has experienced a recent disappointment or rejection. This is because even normal adolescents think in black-and-white terms. They often cannot easily picture a different future and tend to be impulsive.

❑ *Warning signs:*
People who are considering taking their own lives will often give warning signs or signals. Keep in mind that one sign alone does not mean that a person will commit suicide. A combination of several signs, however, may tell you that the person is seeking help. Some common signs are:
- Direct Statements like "I want to die," and "I don't want to live anymore."
- Indirect statements like "I want to go to sleep and never wake up," "They'll be sorry when I'm gone," and "Soon this pain will be over."
- Depression: feeling of loss, hopelessness, helplessness, loneliness, isolation, increase or decrease in sleeping patterns, withdrawal from usual social activities, loss of interest, or a new concern about grades by a poor student.
- Sudden energy following a depression. (Energy is needed to commit suicide.)
- Making final arrangements (giving away possessions, saying good-bye, etc.)
- Increased risk taking (reckless driving, etc.) and frequent accidents.
- Personality changes, such as withdrawal, apathy, and moodiness.
- Themes of death and dying in a person's writing and artwork.
- Marked hostility to those around him or her.
- A detailed plan of how they want to die.

❑ *What can you do?*
Remember that when God created man, one of the first things God noted was that "It is not good that the man should be alone" (Genesis 2:18). It is especially true in the case of acute pain and grief felt by a person who is considering suicide.

   The best help you can provide is to simply *be with that person until we can get them help.* It may not seem like much, but walking along with someone when they are in their darkest moments, easing their load if only for a little while, can mean the difference between life and death.

❑ *Ways to simply "be" with someone:*
- **Show understanding** and acknowledge your concerns through "I" statements.

- **Say** you believe there is some way to ease his or her suffering and in time, to build his or her sense of hope again.
- **Listen** without criticism.
- **Give** support even when you do not support his or her behavior.
- **Ask** about feelings. Try out a few words which express your feelings as if you were in this situation.
- **Validate** the person's feelings and statements so that that peson knows that he or she is being heard by you.
- **Feelings** are not right or wrong. They are feelings.

❑ *Emergency intervention:*
Suicidal feelings, thoughts, impulses, or behaviors should always be taken seriously. If you are thinking about hurting or killing yourself, **SEEK HELP IMMEDIATELY**.

If someone you know has thoughts about suicide, your continued involvement can make a world of difference, so you should try to support them and walk with them in their pain. Ultimately, the very best thing you can do is help him or her get professional help, and stay involved after he or she has gotten that help.

Some Things Your Congregation Can Do Now to Help Encourage Resilience

- Since people who feel known and valued do better in the face of all kinds of stress, consider adopting practices that reduce anonymity and isolation. These can include the following:
  - Providing name tags for everyone at the Oneg Shabbat.
  - Inviting congregants who are *not* active in the synagogue to have honors or read prayers during services.
  - Sending personal birthday and anniversary notes to members inviting the celebrant to join clergy, educators, and/or lay leaders for tea or coffee after services.
- Be creative, consistent, and determined to create a space of greater welcome and intimacy.
- Introduce the principles of resilience including naming and validating emotions in teacher training sessions in your early childhood program and your religious school.
- Invite youth group leaders to participate.
- Invite those who lead and plan programs for all ages and aspects of synagogue life to participate.
- Offer workshops for parents and teens on relaxation, stress reduction, and expressive arts, such as Jewish meditation, noncompetitive sports, exercise classes, yoga, and Jewish journaling classes.
- Try to integrate some of the the above approaches into regular school curriculum.
- In this same spirit, organize health fairs and healthy congregation programs with an emphasis on good nutrition, exercise, and healthy sleep habits, all with a Judaic focus.
- Take an honest look at which foods are served at synagogue events—from Brotherhood Brunches to pre–religious school pizza hours—and make an effort to offer healthier foods in an attractive and appealing way.
- Reduce the stress on achieving perfection and the overvaluing of competition by reviewing your synagogue bulletin and offering alternatives to columns like "We Point with Pride" and "*Nachas* News." Some ideas for alternative columns include interviews of people of all ages. Interview topics can include special birthdays, interviews with families at transition points, families new to the community, men and women who have switched career paths or become involved in new hobbies, new grandparents, couples who have

found one another in midlife, and young people who have opted for a year off before or during college.

- Be certain to mention the very real challenges and points of pain in people's lives in services, during school orientation, and in bulletin articles. People feel less isolated and more able to use prayer and community as sources of support and meaning when they hear their real concerns addressed.

- This does not mean revealing or inviting others to reveal personal problems; this does mean saying something like, "Some of us are struggling with serious depression," "Some of us and some of our kids feel trapped in an eating disorder," or "Some of us are uncertain whether our marriages will survive."

- Of course we don't want to mention all challenges and points of pain at once, but we do want to make our communities ones of compassion and candor, rather than ones of kvelling and covering up.

Section 3

Text Studies

Introduction to Text Studies

The text studies in this section speak to a variety of issues such as the struggles and uncertainties of adolescence, the difficulty some people feel with expressing their emotions, and the influence of the culture of perfectionism upon both teens and adults. The Department of Jewish Family Concerns provides these text studies as examples of the kinds of texts that can spark meaningful discussion about how to strengthen our young adults and families to better cope with the pressures of adolescence.

You may wish to use the text studies that follow as they are written, or they may encourage you to create your own examples based on your greater knowledge of and familiarity with your congregation. Leaders may present these text studies alone or as part of a larger presentation, teach them as lessons, turn them into a sermon, hand parts of them out as part of a pamphlet, etc.

The format of these texts is meant to help you adapt them to your needs. Each chapter in this section begins with an introduction that gives an overview of the topic, followed by the actual texts, which are framed so they may be easily photocopied, cut out, and made into handouts. Each textual segment is then followed by analytical questions meant to stimulate conversation. We recommend that you read through each topic in its entirety first, in order to determine what you would like to focus on.

However used, we recommend breaking larger audiences into smaller groups to discuss the questions presented in a setting where participants may feel more confident about sharing. All participants should feel safe and comfortable with the information they share in these groups. We hope these text studies will be of benefit to you as you integrate resilience-building approaches into your synagogue, and that they help deepen your conversations about strengthening adolescents and supporting their families.

Wandering in the Wilderness

Why Adolescence Is So Difficult

The following texts deal with the biblical account of the Israelites' wandering in the desert. One way to read this narrative is as a tale of developmental transition, the quintessential story of adolescence. The Israelites, having just left the time of dependence and security in Egypt, a period that can be imagined as childhood, spend many years wandering in the wilderness. The wilderness years are a time of confusion, growth, and repeated stumbling as the Israelites move toward a time of full acceptance of responsibility and beginning their rooted life on their own land in Israel, the much anticipated period of adulthood.

The special challenges of this wandering period include rebelliousness and questioning of authority, struggles with hunger and thirst, longing for a home that was lost, feelings of abandonment in the face of rapid change, impulsive behavior in an attempt to deal with overwhelming emotions, substantial emotional growth, and learning to sustain and provide for oneself in the face of hardships and pain. Examining the experience of the wandering "adolescent" Israelites not only helps us better understand the experience of contemporary adolescents, but also gives us insight as to what is needed in order to sustain people in this part of their life journey.

Exodus 17:1–6 (for an alternative text you may choose to use Exodus 16:1–5)

א וַיִּסְעוּ כָּל־עֲדַת בְּנֵי־יִשְׂרָאֵל מִמִּדְבַּר־סִין לְמַסְעֵיהֶם עַל־פִּי
יְהוָה וַיַּחֲנוּ בִּרְפִידִים וְאֵין מַיִם לִשְׁתֹּת הָעָם: ב וַיָּרֶב הָעָם עִם־מֹשֶׁה
וַיֹּאמְרוּ תְּנוּ־לָנוּ מַיִם וְנִשְׁתֶּה וַיֹּאמֶר לָהֶם מֹשֶׁה מַה־תְּרִיבוּן עִמָּדִי
מַה־תְּנַסּוּן אֶת־יְהוָה: ג וַיִּצְמָא שָׁם הָעָם לַמַּיִם וַיָּלֶן הָעָם עַל־מֹשֶׁה וַיֹּאמֶר
לָמָּה זֶּה הֶעֱלִיתָנוּ מִמִּצְרַיִם לְהָמִית אֹתִי וְאֶת־בָּנַי וְאֶת־מִקְנַי בַּצָּמָא:
ד וַיִּצְעַק מֹשֶׁה אֶל־יְהוָה לֵאמֹר מָה אֶעֱשֶׂה לָעָם הַזֶּה עוֹד מְעַט וּסְקָלֻנִי:

45

ה וַיֹּאמֶר יְהֹוָה אֶל־מֹשֶׁה עֲבֹר לִפְנֵי הָעָם וְקַח אִתְּךָ מִזִּקְנֵי יִשְׂרָאֵל וּמַטְּךָ

אֲשֶׁר הִכִּיתָ בּוֹ אֶת־הַיְאֹר קַח בְּיָדְךָ וְהָלָכְתָּ: ו הִנְנִי עֹמֵד לְפָנֶיךָ שָּׁם |

עַל־הַצּוּר בְּחֹרֵב וְהִכִּיתָ בַצּוּר וְיָצְאוּ מִמֶּנּוּ מַיִם וְשָׁתָה הָעָם וַיַּעַשׂ כֵּן מֹשֶׁה

לְעֵינֵי זִקְנֵי יִשְׂרָאֵל:

From the wilderness of Sin the whole Israelite community continued by stages as the Eternal would command. They encamped at Rephidim, and there was no water for the people to drink. The people quarreled with Moses. "Give us water to drink," they said; and Moses replied to them, "Why do you quarrel with me? Why do you try the Eternal?" But the people thirsted there for water; and the people grumbled against Moses and said, "Why did you bring us up from Egypt, to kill us and our children and livestock with thirst?" Moses cried out to the Eternal, saying, "What shall I do with this people? Before long they will be stoning me!" Then the Eternal One said to Moses, "Pass before the people; take with you some of the elders of Israel, and take along the rod with which you struck the Nile, and set out. I will be standing there before you on the rock at Horeb. Strike the rock and water will issue from it, and the people will drink." And Moses did so in the sight of the elders of Israel.

Questions

- Difficulties with food and drink are often experienced in adolescence (problems with alcohol, anorexia, binge eating, experimenting with food ranging from veganism to junk foodism). What can we learn from the people's grumbling, "give us water to drink," about hunger and thirst in the wilderness of adolescence? What thoughts do you have about the meaning of food to people when they are venturing away from the familiar?
- Adolescence is often a time of yearning back toward childhood (even as the young person might not be able to admit such yearnings). What might these texts tell us about why that is? Have you come across this behavior in your experience with adolescents?
  What are some of the pitfalls in remaining in the childhood phase in the wilderness? What are some of the advantages?
- Rebelling and grumbling is a central part of the Israelite experience in the wilderness. What does our text teach us about it? What developmental role do you think rebellion plays?
- How do God and Moses respond? If you dared to rewrite the story (thinking of what you may have wished for from Moses or God if you were one of the grumbling Israelites), what would that response be?
- What is your experience as a parent or leader of youth in regard to teenage rebelliousness? What feelings does this kind of behavior elicit in you? Can you empathize with Moses and God as depicted in the text? What have you found to be effective, as well as ineffective in dealing with the rebelliousness and with your own reactions to it?
- Adolescence is also a time of being sustained in the wilderness. Our texts repeatedly demonstrate the power of nurturance after slavery is left behind. What can we learn about adolescent need from the magical demonstration of nurturance in the text above? Is there some way that we might be able to create experiences for adolescents (or even for ourselves!) where they are able to regress a bit and feel taken care of in ways that seem mag-

ical and strengthening and that teach them how to self-nurture? How might this look in real life in a youth program, family, or synagogue?

- Moses continues to lead and shepherd the Israelites despite moments of wishing to abandon the task. God's continued presence and provision enables the Israelites to move forward, knowing they are never completely alone. What are ways that you (as a parent at home) or the programs you develop (in the synagogue) can offer symbolic demonstration and tangible proof that neither God nor you have left adolescents and young adults to fend entirely for themselves?

Exodus 32:1–6

א וַיַּרְא הָעָם כִּי־בֹשֵׁשׁ מֹשֶׁה לָרֶדֶת מִן־הָהָר וַיִּקָּהֵל הָעָם עַל־אַהֲרֹן וַיֹּאמְרוּ
אֵלָיו קוּם | עֲשֵׂה־לָנוּ אֱלֹהִים אֲשֶׁר יֵלְכוּ לְפָנֵינוּ כִּי־זֶה | מֹשֶׁה הָאִישׁ אֲשֶׁר
הֶעֱלָנוּ מֵאֶרֶץ מִצְרַיִם לֹא יָדַעְנוּ מֶה־הָיָה לוֹ: ב וַיֹּאמֶר אֲלֵהֶם אַהֲרֹן פָּרְקוּ
נִזְמֵי הַזָּהָב אֲשֶׁר בְּאָזְנֵי נְשֵׁיכֶם בְּנֵיכֶם וּבְנֹתֵיכֶם וְהָבִיאוּ אֵלָי:
ג וַיִּתְפָּרְקוּ כָּל־הָעָם אֶת־נִזְמֵי הַזָּהָב אֲשֶׁר בְּאָזְנֵיהֶם וַיָּבִיאוּ אֶל־אַהֲרֹן:
ד וַיִּקַּח מִיָּדָם וַיָּצַר אֹתוֹ בַּחֶרֶט וַיַּעֲשֵׂהוּ עֵגֶל מַסֵּכָה וַיֹּאמְרוּ אֵלֶּה אֱלֹהֶיךָ יִשְׂרָאֵל אֲשֶׁר
הֶעֱלוּךָ מֵאֶרֶץ מִצְרָיִם: ה וַיַּרְא אַהֲרֹן וַיִּבֶן מִזְבֵּחַ לְפָנָיו וַיִּקְרָא אַהֲרֹן וַיֹּאמַר
חַג לַיהוָה מָחָר: ו וַיַּשְׁכִּימוּ מִמָּחֳרָת וַיַּעֲלוּ עֹלֹת וַיַּגִּשׁוּ שְׁלָמִים וַיֵּשֶׁב הָעָם
לֶאֱכֹל וְשָׁתוֹ וַיָּקֻמוּ לְצַחֵק:

When the people saw that Moses was so long in coming down from the mountain, the people gathered against Aaron and said to him, "Come, make us a god who shall go before us, for that man Moses, who brought us from the land of Egypt—we do not know what has happened to him." Aaron said to them, "[You men,] take off the gold rings that are on the ears of your wives, your sons and your daughters, and bring them to me." And all the people took off the gold rings that were in their ears and brought them to Aaron. This he took from them and cast in a mold, and made it into a molten calf. And they exclaimed, "This is your god, O Israel, who brought you out of the land of Egypt!" When Aaron saw this, he built an altar before it; and Aaron announced: "Tomorrow shall be a festival of the Eternal!" Early next day, the people offered up burnt offerings and brought sacrifices of well-being; they sat down to eat and drink, and then rose to dance.

Questions

- Many commentators have speculated as to why the people turned to idolatry while Moses is gone from their midst. What do you think? Adolescence can be a time of turning impulsively to empty—but temporarily distracting, soothing, or exhilarating—sources of comfort. What examples of this kind of behavior have you encountered among teens and adults?

- The Israelites who have only recently left slavery behind, are not yet able to create a new independent identity for themselves. How is this situation similar/dissimilar to what you've encountered among youth, at home, in the synagogue, in the youth group, and elsewhere? How have you dealt with it?

- The text suggests that the Israelites turn from anxiety and sadness to eating, drinking, and dancing. How might this text help parents, campus representatives, and camp administrators understand the degree of partying and drinking among newly independent college-age youth?

- How might Aaron respond differently to their distress? What might help?

- In light of this text, how might we (parents, campus representatives, and camp administrators) better respond to disturbing scenes of revelry that seem to be destructive and defiant? This might include how we respond to the behavior of teens or when we are reflecting upon our own indiscretions.

Exodus 33:13–15, 18–20

יג וְעַתָּ֡ה אִם־נָא֩ מָצָ֨אתִי חֵ֜ן בְּעֵינֶ֗יךָ הוֹדִעֵ֤נִי נָא֙ אֶת־דְּרָכֶ֔ךָ וְאֵדָ֣עֲךָ֔ לְמַ֥עַן

אֶמְצָא־חֵ֖ן בְּעֵינֶ֑יךָ וּרְאֵ֕ה כִּ֥י עַמְּךָ֖ הַגּ֥וֹי הַזֶּֽה׃ יד וַיֹּאמַ֑ר פָּנַ֥י יֵלֵ֖כוּ וַהֲנִחֹ֥תִי לָֽךְ׃

טו וַיֹּ֖אמֶר אֵלָ֑יו אִם־אֵ֤ין פָּנֶ֙יךָ֙ הֹלְכִ֔ים אַֽל־תַּעֲלֵ֖נוּ מִזֶּֽה׃

"Now, if I [Moses] have truly gained Your favor, pray let me know Your ways, that I may know You and continue in Your favor. Consider, too, that this nation is Your people." And [God] said, "I will go in the lead and will lighten your burden." And he replied, "Unless You go in the lead, do not make us leave this place."

יח וַיֹּאמַ֑ר הַרְאֵ֥נִי נָ֖א אֶת־כְּבֹדֶֽךָ׃ יט וַיֹּ֗אמֶר אֲנִ֨י אַעֲבִ֤יר

כָּל־טוּבִי֙ עַל־פָּנֶ֔יךָ וְקָרָ֧אתִֽי בְשֵׁ֛ם יְהֹוָ֖ה לְפָנֶ֑יךָ וְחַנֹּתִי֙ אֶת־אֲשֶׁ֣ר אָחֹ֔ן

וְרִחַמְתִּ֖י אֶת־אֲשֶׁ֥ר אֲרַחֵֽם׃ כ וַיֹּ֕אמֶר לֹ֥א תוּכַ֖ל לִרְאֹ֣ת אֶת־פָּנָ֑י כִּ֛י לֹֽא־יִרְאַ֥נִי

הָאָדָ֖ם וָחָֽי׃

He [Moses] said, "Oh, let me behold Your Presence!" And [God] answered, "I will make all My goodness pass before you, and I will proclaim before you the name Eternal, and the grace that I grant and the compassion that I show," continuing, "But you cannot see My face, for a human being may not see Me and live."

Questions

- Moses seems to feel that he cannot lead unless the people see he is connected to something of eternal meaning. Do you think this is a kind of connection that is necessary in your work with teens, or in your experience with teens at home?

- What are the ways in which those of us who parent youth or who lead youth help them to see us (and themselves) as connected to something more than our own goals?
- What might we learn from Moses's reminder to God, "Consider, too, that this nation is Your people"? What is it Moses teaches us about our role as parents and leaders in relation to our teens?
- Adolescence is a time when teens have a need to really understand those who lead them. From the second text we learn that God only reveals certain aspects of God's self to Moses. Can you relate to this struggle to decide what is an appropriate level of sharing of one's self with adolescents?
- What might be some of the advantages and disadvantages of letting adolescents "see our face"? Is there a difference between "seeing face" and "beholding presence"? If we share a lot of personal information or experiences, we might influence kids unduly or get them so mesmerized by us that they do not engage appropriately in finding their own way.
- What are ways that we can help adolescents "behold our presence" without "seeing our face"?
- What are some of the ways you can think of in which adolescents can learn from us without being overshadowed or overpowered by us?
- What are some ideas you have about applying what we have discussed in these text studies? How can we recognize the overwhelming emotions of our adolescents in the wilderness and provide them with well-timed nourishment, as well as models of living well?

Exodus 16:31–33

לא וַיִּקְרְא֧וּ בֵית־יִשְׂרָאֵ֛ל אֶת־שְׁמ֖וֹ מָ֑ן וְה֗וּא כְּזֶ֤רַע גַּד֙
לָבָ֔ן וְטַעְמ֖וֹ כְּצַפִּיחִ֥ת בִּדְבָֽשׁ: לב וַיֹּ֣אמֶר מֹשֶׁ֗ה זֶ֤ה הַדָּבָר֙ אֲשֶׁ֣ר צִוָּ֣ה יְהֹוָ֔ה
מְלֹ֤א הָעֹ֙מֶר֙ מִמֶּ֔נּוּ לְמִשְׁמֶ֖רֶת לְדֹרֹתֵיכֶ֑ם | לְמַ֣עַן | יִרְא֣וּ אֶת־הַלֶּ֗חֶם אֲשֶׁ֨ר
הֶאֱכַ֤לְתִּי אֶתְכֶם֙ בַּמִּדְבָּ֔ר בְּהוֹצִיאִ֥י אֶתְכֶ֖ם מֵאֶ֥רֶץ מִצְרָֽיִם: לג וַיֹּ֨אמֶר מֹשֶׁ֜ה
אֶֽל־אַהֲרֹ֗ן קַ֚ח צִנְצֶ֣נֶת אַחַ֔ת וְתֶן־שָׁ֥מָּה מְלֹֽא־הָעֹ֖מֶר מָ֑ן וְהַנַּ֤ח אֹתוֹ֙ לִפְנֵ֣י
יְהֹוָ֔ה לְמִשְׁמֶ֖רֶת לְדֹרֹתֵיכֶֽם:

The house of Israel named it manna; it was like coriander seed, white, and it tasted like wafers in honey. Moses said, "This is what the Eternal has commanded: Let one *omer* of it be kept throughout the ages, in order that they may see the bread that I fed you in the wilderness when I brought you out from the land of Egypt." And Moses said to Aaron, "Take a jar, put one *omer* of manna in it, and place it before the Eternal, to be kept throughout the ages."

Questions

- The text reminds us of the sweetness of getting just what you need when you are feeling desperate. How do you decide when it is important to provide for teens rather than pushing them to seek it on their own?

- What symbolic and powerful signs of ongoing sustenance can we provide for teens?
- Adolescence is a time of being sustained in the desert. What future benefits can this sustenance give our teens aside from immediate relief? In other words, why save a sample of the manna?
- What could help our young people remember that they have been nurtured, so that they can have hope during barren times in their lives?

Conclusion

So why is adolescence so difficult? Because it can feel like a long, circular journey in an arid desert. Because it is endlessly confusing. Because it is a time of striving for independence as well as yearning back toward childhood. Because it is a time of struggling with various hungers and with thirst, without yet having gained the necessary skills to deal with those needs and without yet having the long-term perspective that reassures us that we will eventually persevere. Adolescence is difficult because it is a time of rebellion *and* a time of dependence; it is a time of a deep need for love and care despite anger and denial of attachment, a time when teens need desperately to understand those who lead them, as well as to keep them at bay, slightly mysterious and out of reach.

The kind of sustenance that we, as parents and leaders of teens, can provide in this stage of life is crucial. Learning early on how to nourish the self in healthy, safe, and nurturing ways is a lesson that will last through life's many journeys. Our teens do not need us to be perfect or to always have the sagest advice; they derive little benefit from us when we are standing atop a mountain, even if it is in order to converse directly with God. Instead, they need to feel that we are there. Sure, sometimes it seems that it takes a miracle or two to grab their attention, but more than anything, what we as parents and leaders can give our children is a model of how to live well, providing a sense of connectedness to something bigger than the individual self—to family, to community, and to the transcendent in us all.

Walk in My Ways and Be Blameless

Striving for Perfection in an Imperfect World

This text study chapter deals with the commonly shared feeling that we have to be perfect to be worthy of love. While we may know it isn't a feasible expectation, or for that matter, that it isn't really demanded of us, many of us fall prey to perfectionism's powerful grip. Within Judaism, perfection has never been considered a possibility for human beings. Even our greatest prophets, Moses among them, had all too human flaws. If the lesson we draw from the Bible is that God's love depends on our perfection, we fundamentally misread our tradition, which not only acknowledges our limitations as human beings, but is capable of seeing them as opportunities for growth, whereby flaws are turned into unique advantages. When we fail to meet our own or others' expectations of perfection, Judaism does not teach that we need to punish ourselves or deny ourselves pleasures until we eventually succeed; rather, we are taught to acknowledge our humanity, to embrace our strengths, and accept our weaknesses, for they too are a part of God's blessing for us.

Bava Batra 60b

אֵין גּוֹזְרִין גְּזֵירָה עַל הַצִּבּוּר אֶלָּא אִם כֵּן רוֹב הַצִּבּוּר יְכוֹלִין לַעֲמוֹד בָּהּ.

Our Rabbis taught that when the Temple was destroyed the second time [by the Romans in 70 C.E.] many Jews separated themselves and no longer ate meat or drank wine. Rabbi Yehoshua met with them and said: "My children, why are you not eating meat or drinking wine?" They replied: "Shall we eat meat when the altar they used to offer up sacrifices upon is no more? Shall we drink wine when the altar they used to pour wine upon is no more?" Rabbi Yehoshua responded: "If this is your reasoning, then we should not eat bread for the meal offerings also have ceased." The separatists then raised the possibility of just eating fruit. Rabbi Yehoshua answered: "We cannot

---

eat fruit either for the offering of the First Fruits has also ceased." The separatists then raised the possibility of just eating other kinds of fruits not offered at the Temple. Rabbi Yehoshua responded: "Then we cannot drink water for the water libation [at the Temple] has also ceased." The separatists were silenced. Rabbi Yehoshua continued: "My children, come and I will instruct you. Not to mourn at all is impossible for the decree against the Temple has been issued. Yet to mourn too much is also impossible for we may not impose a decree upon the community unless most of the community is able to comply with it."

Genesis 17:1

וַיְהִי אַבְרָם בֶּן־תִּשְׁעִים שָׁנָה וְתֵשַׁע שָׁנִים וַיֵּרָא יְהֹוָה אֶל־אַבְרָם וַיֹּאמֶר
אֵלָיו אֲנִי־אֵל שַׁדַּי הִתְהַלֵּךְ לְפָנַי וֶהְיֵה תָמִים:

When Abram was 99 years old, the Eternal appeared to Abram and said to him, "I am El Shaddai—walk in my ways and be blameless."

Questions

- What aspect of human character do you think the Rabbis were responding to when they prohibited excessive mourning and self-denial?
- How do you interpret God's charge to Abraham to be *tamim*, blameless?
- What are some ways that you know of, from your life experience, in which you or those around you try and be *tamim*? Is the process positive or negative? Are the results?
- Do the texts above contradict or compliment each other?
- Does Judaism provide any example of people who found love and forgiveness despite their imperfections?
- In your experience, does Jewish culture, as opposed to Jewish tradition, encourage or discourage the striving for perfection?
- Is there a difference between the pursuit for excellence and perfectionism? What do you think the difference is?

Exodus 4:10–16

י וַיֹּאמֶר מֹשֶׁה אֶל־יְהוָה בִּי אֲדֹנָי לֹא
אִישׁ דְּבָרִים אָנֹכִי גַּם מִתְּמוֹל גַּם מִשִּׁלְשֹׁם גַּם מֵאָז דַּבֶּרְךָ אֶל־עַבְדֶּךָ כִּי

כְּבַד־פֶּה וּכְבַד לָשׁוֹן אָנֹכִי: יא וַיֹּאמֶר יְהֹוָה אֵלָיו מִי שָׂם פֶּה לָאָדָם אוֹ

מִי־יָשׂוּם אִלֵּם אוֹ חֵרֵשׁ אוֹ פִקֵּחַ אוֹ עִוֵּר הֲלֹא אָנֹכִי יְהֹוָה: יב וְעַתָּה לֵךְ

וְאָנֹכִי אֶהְיֶה עִם־פִּיךָ וְהוֹרֵיתִיךָ אֲשֶׁר תְּדַבֵּר: יג וַיֹּאמֶר בִּי אֲדֹנָי שְׁלַח־נָא

בְּיַד־תִּשְׁלָח: יד וַיִּחַר־אַף יְהֹוָה בְּמֹשֶׁה וַיֹּאמֶר הֲלֹא אַהֲרֹן אָחִיךָ הַלֵּוִי

יָדַעְתִּי כִּי־דַבֵּר יְדַבֵּר הוּא וְגַם הִנֵּה־הוּא יֹצֵא לִקְרָאתֶךָ וְרָאֲךָ וְשָׂמַח בְּלִבּוֹ:

טו וְדִבַּרְתָּ אֵלָיו וְשַׂמְתָּ אֶת־הַדְּבָרִים בְּפִיו וְאָנֹכִי אֶהְיֶה עִם־פִּיךָ וְעִם־פִּיהוּ

וְהוֹרֵיתִי אֶתְכֶם אֵת אֲשֶׁר תַּעֲשׂוּן: טז וְדִבֶּר־הוּא לְךָ אֶל־הָעָם וְהָיָה הוּא

יִהְיֶה־לְּךָ לְפֶה וְאַתָּה תִּהְיֶה־לּוֹ לֵאלֹהִים:

But Moses said to the Eternal, "Please, O my lord, I have never been a man of words, either in times past or now that You have spoken to Your servant; I am slow of speech and slow of tongue." And the Eternal said to him, "Who gives humans speech? Who makes them dumb or deaf, seeing or blind? Is it not I, the Eternal? Now go, and I will be with you as you speak and will instruct you what to say." But he said, "Please, O my lord, make someone else Your agent." The Eternal became angry with Moses and said, "There is your brother Aaron the Levite. He, I know, speaks readily. Even now he is setting out to meet you, and he will be happy to see you. You shall speak to him and put the words in his mouth—I will be with you and with him as you speak, and tell both of you what to do—and he shall speak for you to the people. Thus he shall serve as your spokesman, with you playing the role of God to him."

Questions

- There are many commentaries regarding the meaning of Moses being *kvad peh ukvad lashon*, slow of speech, and slow of tongue. Some commentators argue that Moses had a severe stutter. Some say he forgot how to speak the language of Egypt. Some say he could not pronounce certain letters, or that he did not express himself smoothly and had trouble finding the right words. What in your opinion is Moses trying to tell God when he says he is *kvad peh ukvad lashon*?

- Why does God insist on placing Moses in the ultimate leadership role when his qualifications are less than perfect? What benefit is there in "employing" someone who is not a "man of words," who is "slow of speech and slow of tongue" in a position of public speaking?

- What can we learn from God's proclamation, "Who gives humans speech? Who makes them dumb or deaf, seeing or blind? Is it not I, the Eternal?" Do imperfections play an important role? In other words, if it is clearly in God's power to remove Moses's speech impediment, why doesn't God do so?

- Can you think of a time or a context in your own life experience (or those around you) in which you felt you gained something deep from having flaws and imperfections you would not have otherwise gained?

- God does not reassure Moses that he is indeed a good speaker. Rather, he acknowledges that he is not by pointing out Aaron, who is, and will therefore serve as mouthpiece to

Moses. Have you ever faced a situation where you had to respond to a child who did not perform to his or her own or other's expectations? How did you react?

• Instead of "fixing" Moses up with the right skills so that he would be perfect for the task, God wants Moses to receive help where help is needed, to be completed by another where he is lacking. What do both Moses and Aaron stand to gain from their collaboration?

After discussing the above texts, consider dividing your audience into smaller discussion groups of six to eight people. Each group should read the following additional texts. After doing so, the discussion leader might pose the questions that follow the texts.

Further Discussion

My candidate for the most important single word in the Bible occurs in Genesis 17:1, when God says to Abraham, "Walk before Me and be tamim." What does that word mean? The King James Bible translates it as "perfect"; the Revised Standard version takes it to mean "blameless." . . . My own study of the verse leads me to conclude that what God wants from Abraham, and by implication from us, is not perfection, but integrity. God wants Abraham to strive to be true to the core of who he is, even if he strays from that core occasionally. As the folk saying puts it, "I'm not much, Lord, but I'm all I've got." Or as Mother Teresa once told an interviewer, "We are not here to be successful; we are here to be faithful," which I would take to mean faithful to our essential selves as well as to God.

Harold Kushner, *How Good Do We Have To Be? A New Understanding of Guilt and Forgiveness* (Boston: Little Brown, 1996), p. 169.

Within Judaism you can find an antidote to the "special-itis" our culture fosters. Judaism asks that we raise our children not in the hope that they are the Messiah but to be themselves. Consider the wisdom of Rabbi Zusya, an early Hasidic leader and folk hero. Zusya was known as a modest and benevolent man who, despite his meager knowledge of Torah, attained merit because of his innocence and personal righteousness. Before he died he said, "When I reach the world to come, God will not ask me why I wasn't more like Moses. He will ask me why I wasn't more like Zusya."

Wendy Mogel, *The Blessing of a Skinned Knee: Using Jewish Teachings to Raise Self-Reliant Children* (New York, Penguin, 2001), p. 50.

Questions

• Do you feel pressure to be perfect in some or all aspects of your life? If so, how much of that pressure comes from others and how much from yourself?
• How do you react when you fail to meet expectations, either others or your own?
• How do you think making a mistake affects how others see you? How do you react when a friend makes a mistake?
• Describe a time when you were able to shake off a mistake.
• Describe a time when you were unable to accept a mistake.
• What does it mean on a personal level to acknowledge our imperfection?

To Free the Captive

Helping Someone Is Not Always Easy

The first text study in this chapter expresses the traditional Jewish view that a captive cannot break free from captivity on his or her own. Only someone who stands outside the prison can redeem the captive. When we do so, we do holy work. As part of the morning service we say:

בָּרוּךְ אַתָּה יהוה אֱלֹהֵינוּ מֶלֶךְ הָעוֹלָם מַתִּיר אֲסוּרִים.

"Blessed are you, *Adonai*, Sovereign of the Universe, who frees the captive."

This blessing reminds us that part of our obligation as Jews requires us to redeem those in captivity. This obligation extends beyond those actually locked up. It includes those suffering all kinds of confining physical illness, as well as those trapped in destructive ways of thinking about themselves that can bind human beings as tightly as any actual shackle.

In discussing our obligation to redeem the captive, we also need to consider circumstances in which the prison actually provides a sense of comfort or relief from affliction. When someone cuts herself, or drinks until he gets sick, instead of turning our backs on that person because we feel he or she has chosen to engage in destructive behavior, we may, instead, be able to see his or her affliction as a prison; his or her behaviors as shackles that, although self-imposed, still hold that peson captive.

Talmud Bavli, Berachot 5b

Rabbi Chiya bar Abba was sick. Rabbi Yochanan went to visit him and asked Rabbi Chiya: "Are these afflictions dear to you?" Rabbi Chiya answered: "Neither they nor their reward." Rabbi Yochanan said to him: "Give me your hand." Rabbi Chiya gave him his hand and Rabbi Yochanan revived him.

Rabbi Yochanan was then ill. Rabbi Chanina went to him and asked: "Are these afflictions dear to you?" Rabbi Yochanan answered: "Neither they nor their reward." Rabbi Chanina responded: "Give me your hand." Rabbi Yochanan gave him his hand and Rabbi Chanina revived him.

> Why [did Rabbi Yochanan need Rabbi Chanina's extended hand]? Rabbi Yochanan should have revived himself! The Sages replied: "A captive cannot free himself from a prison."

Questions

- When the Sages say that their "afflictions are not dear" to them, what do you think they mean?
- Are people ever happy with their afflictions?
- Is it true that we sometimes find it easier to heal others than ourselves? If so, why do you think that is?
- In what ways do we make ourselves captives? What are the signs of captivity in others and ourselves?
- Why do you think Rabbi Yochanan took Rabbi Chanina's hand? Do you think it was easy for him to do so?
- When someone reaches out to us in our own prisons, are we always eager to take their hand? If not, what are the obstacles that prevent us from accepting help from others?
- Can our refusal to accept help on some occasions be another form of captivity? Or is it just healthy self-reliance?
- How do we decide when to extend a hand and when to respect someone else's privacy?
- When the person we try to help reacts with anger or resentment, how should we respond?

Rambam (Maimonides): Mishneh Torah, Gifts to the Poor 8:10

פִּדְיוֹן שְׁבוּיִים קוֹדֵם לְפַרְנָסַת עֲנִיִּים וּלְכַסּוּתָן, וְאֵין לְךָ מִצְוָה גְּדוֹלָה כְּפִדְיוֹן

שְׁבוּיִים שֶׁהַשָּׁבוּי הֲרֵי הוּא בִּכְלַל הָרְעֵבִים וְהַצְּמֵאִים וְהָעֲרוּמִים וְעוֹמֵד בְּסַכָּנַת נְפָשׁוֹת,

וְהַמַּעֲלִים עֵינָיו מִפִּדְיוֹנוֹ הֲרֵי

זֶה עוֹבֵר עַל "לֹא תְאַמֵּץ אֶת־לְבָבְךָ וְלֹא תִקְפֹּץ אֶת־יָדְךָ" (דְּבָרִים טו, ז), וְעַל "לֹא

תַעֲמֹד עַל־דַּם רֵעֶךָ"

(וַיִּקְרָא יט, טז), וְעַל "לֹא־יִרְדֶּנּוּ בְּפֶרֶךְ לְעֵינֶיךָ" (שָׁם כה, נג) וְעַל מִצְוַת "פָּתֹחַ

תִּפְתַּח אֶת־יָדְךָ לוֹ"

(דְּבָרִים טו, ח) וּמִצְוַת "וְחֵי אָחִיךָ עִמָּךְ" (וַיִּקְרָא כה, לו), "וְאָהַבְתָּ לְרֵעֲךָ כָּמוֹךָ"

(שָׁם יט, יח), וְ" הַצֵּל לְקֻחִים לַמָּוֶת"

(מִשְׁלֵי כד, יא) וְהַרְבֵּה דְּבָרִים כָּאֵלּוּ, וְאֵין לְךָ מִצְוָה רַבָּה כְּפִדְיוֹן שְׁבוּיִים.

The redemption of captives takes precedence over supporting the poor. . . . One who ignores the responsibility to redeem the captive violates the following negative commandments: "do not harden your heart and shut your hand [from your brother in need]" (Deut. 15:7); "do not stand idly by the blood of your neighbor's" (Lev. 19:16);

"the other [the master] shall not rule ruthlessly in your sight " (Lev. 25:53). He similarly annuls a number of positive commandments: "you must open your hand and lend whatever is sufficient to meet the need" (Deut. 15:8); "Let your kin live by your side as such" (Lev. 25:36); "you shall love your neighbor as yourself" (Lev. 19:18); and "deliver them that are drawn unto death" (Prov. 24:11), and many such as those. There is no mitzvah as great as the redemption of captives.

Questions

- How is the plight of hostages in captivity similar to that of those in the bonds of self-inflicted destructive behavior? How is it different?
- The Rambam makes clear that redeeming the captives is a societal obligation in the highest degree. What are the implications of that when we view captives as people who are imprisoned by their own behaviors?
- Which mitzvah do you consider to be the most compelling justification to act on behalf of those who are prisoners of their own self-destructive behaviors?
- Have you ever reached out to help someone who is harming him- or herself or otherwise self-imprisoned in behavior or thought? What was it that moved you to try and "redeem" this person?
- What are the ways in which we sometimes might "harden [our] heart and shut [our] hand" from those in self-destructive captivity?
- What are the ways in which we can surely "open [our] hand" to them?
- What are some of the ways in which we might fulfill our societal obligation to redeem the captives in our own community?

For Additional Study

He who entreats [God's] mercy for his fellow while he himself is in need of the same thing will be answered first, for it is said: "the Lord changed the fortune of Job when he prayed for his friend" (Job 42:10), p. 525.

Hayim Nahman Bialik and Y.H. Ravnitzky,
The Book of Legends/Sefer Ha-Aggadah: Legends from the Talmud and Midrash
(New York: Schocken Books, 1992).

Remember, suicidal people often give warning signs of their intent. They may show signs that they are depressed, always talking about death, and making final arrangements. Generally, a person will show more than one sign at a time. People who talk about suicide **ARE** seriously considering taking their own lives. These people **ARE** "crying" for help and this warning should **NOT** be ignored.

Union for Reform Judaism, "Preventing Youth Suicide," **www.urj.org/jfc**.

One of the more difficult and damaging forms of reaction to self-inflicted violence is non-reaction. Sometimes those around you simply will not respond to your behaviors, leaving you feeling invisible. As stated before, [self-inflicted violence] is often tied to feelings of isolation and alienation. When you are ignored, the feelings of invisibility can lead right back to the feelings of isolation and alienation that are part of the cycle of [self-inflicted violence].

Tracy Alderman, *The Scarred Soul: Understanding & Ending Self-Inflicted Violence*
(Oakland, CA: New Harbinger Publications, 1997), p. 116.

Conclusion

We cannot, admittedly, always notice when someone we care about needs help. We cannot be eternally vigilant, nor can we always expect to make the right decision when balancing our compassion with our respect for another's right of privacy and self-determination. In *Pirkei Avot* we learn that it is not our duty to complete the task, yet we may not desist from it either. All we can hope for is an eye capable of seeing the isolation of others and a hand willing to extend in friendship.

The Binding of Isaac

Images of Sacrifice

Genesis 22:2

וַיֹּאמֶר קַח־נָא אֶת־בִּנְךָ אֶת־יְחִידְךָ אֲשֶׁר־אָהַבְתָּ אֶת־יִצְחָק וְלֶךְ־לְךָ אֶל־אֶרֶץ
הַמֹּרִיָּה וְהַעֲלֵהוּ שָׁם לְעֹלָה עַל אַחַד הֶהָרִים אֲשֶׁר אֹמַר אֵלֶיךָ:

[God] said, "Take your son, your only one, the one you love, Isaac, and go forth to the land of Moriah. Offer him there as a burnt-offering, on one of the mountains that I will show you."

There are many instances in our lives where we believe we are asked to sacrifice something precious to us in order to accomplish or be worthy of something else. The story of the *Akeidah*, the Binding of Isaac, is perhaps the most extreme example of heeding a call to sacrifice in order to prove faithfulness and devotion—in this case, to God.

Many stories in the Torah present us with models of parenting, some good, some bad, but perhaps none more controversial than the Binding of Isaac, where Abraham is willing to raise a knife to slay his own son. In the biblical account, an angel comes at the right moment and tells Abraham to lower his knife, but the story does not really end there; the many midrashim written on the *Akeidah* (some dating as far back as 2,000 years ago, some very recent) suggest there is something eternal in the story of parenthood and sacrifice. Israeli poetry, for example, suggests that the knife, the instrument and symbol of the willingness to destroy that which is most cherished as a way of seeking favor, remains embedded in the psyche of the world forever.

How does the ancient story of Abraham and Isaac relate to our own lives? What can we learn from the way in which the *Akeidah* was perceived both by ancient Rabbis and recent poets? The following texts offer a discussion about the various images of sacrifice. "Sacrificing" is taken to mean giving up something that is dear to us in the pursuit of holiness, or perhaps in order to attain something else we feel is demanded of us, just as God made a demand upon Abraham in order to prove loyalty. What is the price of such sacrifice? How do we know when we are being asked

59

for too much? Are we allowed to raise objections when we do feel the price demanded of us is too high?

Perhaps one of the major lessons we can learn from the *Akeidah* is that in order for us to be able to serve what is central in life, we need to pay close attention to the messages that seem to be "on the front of our monitor." We must learn how to heed those messages we get from our various environments—work, school, religion, general culture, etc., and learn how to heed only those that truly bring holiness into our lives.

Midrash: Tanhuma, Vayeira § 23 / Ecclesiastes Rabbah 9:7 § I

[At the time Isaac was bound], Satan went to Sarah, appearing to her in the form of Isaac. When Sarah saw him, she asked, "My son, what did your father do to you?" He replied, "My father took me, led me up hills and down into valleys, until finally he brought me up to the summit of a high and towering mountain, where he built an altar, set out the firewood, bound me upon the altar, and grasped a knife to cut my throat. Had not the Holy One said to him, 'Lay not thy hand upon the lad,' I would have been slaughtered." Even before Satan finished his tale, Sarah's soul left her.

Questions

- Sarah's first question to Isaac "my son, what did *your* father do to you?" holds a lot of tension relating to differences and conflicts between parents in relation to raising children. Can you think of instances in which parents might disagree over what is harmful or appropriate for their child?

- This subtle portrayal of unresolved family conflict, which Satan preys upon, teaches us something about the deviousness of Satan. More importantly, though, it teaches us how he is able to achieve his goal. Why do you think Satan is so successful in his ploy?

- Note the abundance of action on Abraham's part in the way Satan/Isaac tells the tale. What can we learn from it about how eager we are to "do" in certain circumstances? What is hinted at by Abraham's haste?

- Have you ever found yourself in a situation where you were sacrificing something that made you feel very uneasy? Is there something in this depiction of Abraham's haste, in his multiple actions, that resonates with your experience?

- This midrash is written as Satan's account of the *Akeidah*; as such, Abraham is portrayed in a very negative light. What does it tell us about what the Rabbis thought of the biblical account of the *Akeidah*? What can the choice of Satan as "spokesman" teach us about how hard it is to go against viewing Abraham as a figure to be venerated? How might such a subversive view influence our thinking of the bible?

- Sarah's soul left her *before* Satan finished his story. Given that she *sees* Isaac in front of her, and thus has no reason to suspect there was anything else but a happy ending, why do you think that is?

- Aviva Zornberg explains that Sarah's death is caused by the deep and immediate realization of "that hair's breadth that separates death from life." In other words, Sarah dies because she suddenly grasps what *could* have been. Moments like this can give us a sense of vulnerability, an awareness of how fragile life is, of what terrible things can happen. Perhaps we discover that fathers can indeed kill their sons, that a ferocious faith can lead some people astray, or above all, that death is always looking over our shoulders. Can you think of examples from your own life where you experienced something like this?

Genesis Rabbah 56:8

When I [God] told you "take now your son" . . . Did I tell you "Slaughter him?" Did I not rather tell you "Bring him up?" [a word play on the root *aleph-lamed-hei* in Hebrew]. You brought him up on the altar, now take him down again!"

Questions

• In this midrash, God is said to criticize Abraham for hearing something other than what God intended to say. God's voice then comes down and chastises Abraham, telling him to undo his actions. Think of God's voice as akin to the messages we sometimes hear in our minds. We all have safety devices and mechanisms of self-reflection that help us to double-check our actions and decisions. Can you think of an example where you came close to giving up something you cherish only to have your hand stayed at the last minute?
• Do we sometimes misunderstand our call to sacrifice something?
• The two midrashim above suggest that the Rabbis were very critical of Abraham's act. Their criticism was heard and recorded in the sacred texts of our tradition. We can learn from that, that Judaism "contains" many conflicting voices, as does every human being. How to balance them well is the trick. Can you think of any examples of balancing conflicting voices in your life, or the lives of people you know?

Genesis Rabbah 65:10

"And [Isaac's] eyes were dim from seeing" (Gen 27:1). . . . "From Seeing"—from the effect of what he saw at his binding. When our father Abraham bound his son upon the altar, the ministering angels wept and tears dropped from their eyes into Isaac's eyes, leaving their mark upon them. And when he grew old, his eyes grew dim.

Questions

• What is meant by "what he saw at his binding"?
• What kind of things do you imagine Isaac seeing? Was it the impending doom his father was about to inflict upon him? Was it, perhaps, his father's pain?
• Sometimes we sacrifice something cherished because we believe it is demanded of us. The midrash suggests that we carry the painful memory of such sacrifice with us to old age. Can you think of an example?
• Can you think of other examples when parents think they are pursuing holiness but children end up being sacrificed? Is it possible even for parents who give their children the best education possible, the finest developmental opportunities, and all the comforts they can provide, to still cause their children pain? How?
• When we give up parts of ourselves, or when we sacrifice something cherished, it leaves a mark within us. We all have tears in our eyes when our families are torn apart by a voice

telling us—when it comes to significant, substantial matters—"there's only one way!" Do you think we have a right to question such voices?

Deeds of the Fathers[1]

And after the binding?
Then began the hardest test of all.

Abraham took his son to the camel races
Went hiking with him from the Euphrates to the river Nile,
swam by his side, keeping a close eye
in the waters of Eilat. And upon their return,
he slaughtered herds and sheep aplenty,
all tender and juicy
the scent of songs, and flesh and muscle
and guests in good graces come in from afar.
Isaac ate and ate, and ate
And was silent.

Abraham bought his wife a fur coat,
ornaments of red gold,
installed for her emergency lighting in the tent
brought her boots in style from a shop on the Nile,
hashish from Tarshish,
cinnamon from Lebanon.
Sarah, who withered overnight,
did not remove her mourning clothes.

Abraham prayed to his God morning and evening,
hung tzedakah boxes atop all the cedar trees,
studied his Torah night and day,
fasted,
And lodged angels for almost no pay.
The voice from on high disappeared.

And the voice inside him
(the only one he had left)
said: yes, you went,
from your land, from your homeland, and from your father's house,
and now, finally, from yourself.

---

[1]T. Carmi, *"Maasei Avot"* in: *La'Netsach Anagnech: Ha'Mikra BaShira HaIvrit HaChadasha—Antologia,* ed. Malka Shaked (published in Hebrew). Translation by the URJ Department of Jewish Family Concerns.

Questions

- What do you make of all the merriments in the first stanza? What is Abraham trying to do? Does it work? Have you ever encountered such behavior?
- Why did Sarah not take off her mourning clothes?
- The poem suggests the binding cost Abraham his ability to be connected to himself. Abraham lost his way. Can you think of examples where sacrificing something so important caused someone to lose their way?
- In the poem Abraham is trying to make up with material things for what he did to Isaac. Sometimes, when we are in a lost place in our lives, when our guilt and pain are unassuaged and our emotions are unmanageable, we overindulge. Can you think of examples?
- "The voice from on high disappeared." Why? What is the claim made in the poem about the relationship between Abraham and God? About Abraham "passing" his test? What do you learn from it regarding conforming to demands, either the ones we have of ourselves, or the ones given us by others?

Isaac[2]

The ram came last.
And Abraham didn't know
that it answered the question
that had come first
in the sunset of his life.

When he raised his white head
he saw he was not dreaming;
when he saw the angel
the knife dropped from his hand.

The boy who was unbound
Saw the back of his father.

Isaac, it is told, was not sacrificed.
He had a long life, a good life,
until his eyes went dark.

But that hour
he bequeathed to his descendents
still to be born
a knife
in the heart.

---

[2]Haim Guri, "Isaac," in *Voices Within the Ark—The Modern Jewish Poets*, eds. Howard Schwartz and Anthony Rudolph (New York: Avon Books, 1980), p. 98.

Questions

- According to the poem, the inheritance bequeathed to us by Abraham is "a knife in the heart." What kinds of examples can you think of that exemplify the existence of this knife in our lives, and in our relationships with ourselves and others?
- Note the poem says "Isaac, it is told, was not sacrificed." What do you make of "it is told?" Is there something else hinted here?
- We all cause pain, because we all have pain; hence the knife in our heart. If a mother tells her daughter she's fat, it's probably true that someone else told the mother *she* was fat when she was a girl. How can we get out of this circle and stop perpetuating pain and guilt?
- We might think of the knife in the heart as the voice that "we hear" telling us to hurt ourselves. Have you ever caused yourself pain trying to fulfill something you thought was expected of you?
- What do you make of "the boy . . . saw the back of his father?" Do parents ever turn their backs on their children? Do people ever turn their backs to parts of themselves? Have you ever felt like you were turning your back on a part of yourself?

Conclusion

The *Akeidah* is such a compelling story of parental conduct precisely because it challenges everything that we have come to think of as good parenting. The challenge of the *Akeidah* therefore becomes not heeding the call of God, but listening to it carefully—taking note of the voices that surround us and so often propel us to push for the perfect body; for academic excellence at all costs; or for ignoring our own dreams for ourselves and, in the process, to do violence to what we cherish.

There is no doubt that almost all parents want the best for their children. Every parent is filled with hopes, dreams, and expectations in regard to those beings they have brought into this world and nurtured with great love and care. And yet, it also happens that sometimes, even when parents mean the very best, their own pain prevents them from seeing that their children are being sacrificed on the altar of parental hopes and expectations.

Essentially, we should all remember that "[t]he point of the [*Akeidah*] story is that Abraham didn't kill him. . . . What makes Abraham the father of our people is that he is able to recognize that the voices of accumulated pain are *not* God, and that the real voice of God does *not* want him to sacrifice his child."[3]

---

[3]Michael Lerner, "The Binding of Isaac," *Tikkun* 7, no. 5 (September/October 1992): 7–8.

Section 4

Gathering Information and Facilitating Discussion

Best Practices 1:
Sample Program Materials
from Temple Sinai of Toronto

The involvement of Temple Sinai with *Kedushat HaGuf*[1] begins with one family—two parents, active congregants and lay leaders of Temple Sinai of Toronto—who struggled with their daughter's eating disorder for years. It was when the worst was behind them and their daughter was well on her way to recovery that they realized they had learned so much about adolescent stresses and suffering through their own experiences with their daughter's eating disorder, they simply had to do something about it. Committed to reducing the suffering of others, preventing eating disorders, and helping their treasured community to be a source of support and hope for other families, in 2004 they created an endowment and set about seeking help in reaching their goal. The result was The *Kedushat HaGuf* Project at Temple Sinai of Toronto.

One of the most important developments of the project was the creation of a *Kedushat HaGuf* committee in November 2006. The KHG committee was a development of the already existing Caring Community involved in bringing meals to the sick and responding to the bereaved in the community. In creating this KHG committee the group was in essence broadening its vision to also provide support with "ordinary" pressures and stresses before they lead to breakdown and illness. Members of the KHG committee were pediatricians, teachers, psychologists, and yoga and art specialists, who were all interested in furthering programming around eating disorder education and prevention. The committee members all had personal experience within their family and friendship circles with the various kinds of adolescent stresses and the less than safe responses to them that are of concern. Temple Sinai's Clergy (Rabbi Michael N. Dolgin, Rabbi Lori R. Cohen, Rabbi Erin L. Polonsky, and Cantor Gershon Silins) as well as the Director of Education (Dr. Ira H. Schweitzer) all worked in collaboration with the committee and were crucial contributors to the committee's success.

When the *Kedushat HaGuf* committee was first created with the focus of furthering programming around eating disorders, the members of the KHG committee soon discovered that focusing on the pathological aspects was too threatening for most people.

---

[1]Pilot programs of *Resilience of the Soul* were introduced in congregations under the project's former title, *Kedushat HaGuf*. All references to the project in this document will therefore be under the title of *Kedushat HaGuf.*

Their very first meeting was publicized using bylines such as:

- Learn the Signs: Symptoms and Warning Signs of Eating Disorders or Other Addictions
- Learn about the Resources in the Community to Start/Maintain the Recovery Process

The program did not have the hoped for attendance or effect. Nonetheless, this was a good learning experience for Temple Sinai and can be so for others as well. From the committee's own report: "It seems that although there appeared to be a need . . . the topic was too threatening for our members and we had little to no response. We even advertised to the general community (the Canadian Jewish News had a lovely article plus flyers were sent to Jewish agencies all around Toronto—UJA, JFCS, JCC, and JACS) and it had the same lack of response. We had to reevaluate our focus."

Wiser after their initial experience, the committee decided to change the focus to "making healthy choices dealing with stressful situations."

Below are some sample materials and timetables of the training sessions included in Temple Sinai's project.

Sample Publicity Flier

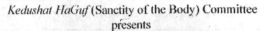

Kedushat HaGuf (Sanctity of the Body) Committee
presents

Rabbi Edythe Held Mencher
Associate Director of the Department of
Jewish Family Concerns of the URJ

Fri. Jan. 26, 2007 at 8.00 p.m.
Kabbalat Shabbat Service
Using Biblical Storytelling to
Create a Community of Support and Encouragement

Sat. Jan. 27, 2007 at 10.00 a.m.
Chevrat Torah Service
Drawing on our Jewish Sources toward
Building a Sense of Self-worth and Resilience
followed by a lunchtime discussion at **12.15 p.m.**

Sun. Jan. 28, 2007 from 10.30 a.m. to 12.00 p.m.
Spiritual Well-being and Stress Reduction
An interactive program for all grade 5 and 6 students and their parents.
Skill-building activities will include communication, nutrition and yoga.

From the Temple Bulletin

KEDUSHAT HAGUF COMMITTEE

<u>Mark your calendars</u>
**Fri. Jan. 26, Sat. Jan. 27
& Sun. Jan. 28**
with
<u>Rabbi Edythe Held Mencher</u>

The Temple Sinai *Kedushat HaGuf* (Sanctity of the Body) Committee is proud to present three days with a little something for everyone!!

o Do we know what pressures and stresses our kids face on a daily basis?
o What methods are available to reduce these stresses in a healthy and respectful manner?
o Do we have the tools to talk openly with our children and teenagers?
o What does our tradition teach us about caring for ourselves emotionally and physically?

Rabbi Edythe Held Mencher,
the Associate Director of the Department of Jewish Family Concerns of the Union for Reform Judaism will be with us for the weekend. Rabbi Mencher has a Master of Social Work degree as well as certification in the study of psychoanalysis and psychotherapy. She has been very involved in the building of communities of caring, seeking to bring together the wisdom of Jewish tradition and the knowledge derived from training as a mental health professional.
Join us on **Fri. Jan. 26, 2007** at **8.00 *p.m.*** at *Kabbalat Shabbot* service. Our topic will be: *How to Build Relationships and Communities Where People Feel Valued and Cherished.*

Our *Shabbat Chevrat Torah* service on **Sat. Jan. 27, 2007 at 10.00 a.m.** will include a text-based study followed by a lunchtime discussion with Rabbi Mencher at **12.15 *p.m.***
On **Sun. Jan. 28, 2007 from 10.30 a.m. to 12.00 *p.m.*** there will be an interactive program for all grade *5* and 6 students and their parents, with Rabbi Mencher, directed toward spiritual well-being.
Parents and youth will have time to study intergenerationally as well as in parallel programs.
Our confirmation students and Hebrew school teaching assistants will also have the opportunity to meet with Rabbi Mencher at informational sessions during the weekend.
For further details watch our Temple Web site www.templesinai.net
And our weekly E-vents@TS flyers.

On Saturday, January 27, 2007, at 12:15, a lunch-discussion program was planned for the staff of Temple Sinai in which Rabbi Mencher answered questions and responded to some concerns. Some notes from that meeting follow:

- Listen and always keep in mind your role, asking, "How can I help as a rabbi, as a cantor, as the Jewish educator, as the synagogue lay leader?" By this I mean establishing that, of course, all of us can listen to the person's distress, but what we can actually do should be *filtered through the lens of our role* so that the congregant and we are clear about resources and limits. Thus, we should refer back to "Jewish tradition suggests, Judaism encourages us to, my experience with other students is . . ." and wherever possible to refer to specific Jewish sources and activities that might be of help to them, linking them to faith in God, to the tradition, and to the community.
- How to make referrals:
  - Why we don't give advice or refer to our own personal experience
  - How to make a referral without inadvertently seeming to wish to send the person to someone else instead of remaining available to them
  - How to make the referral so the person feels that other help is indeed needed, but that we remain a spiritual and communal resource
- Discussion of new rituals in regard to the changing family: some rituals, cards, prayers (familiarizing participants with available materials by the URJ Department of Jewish Family Concerns).

Timetable and Evaluations—From the Committee's Report

Friday, January 26, 2007

Rabbi Mencher arrives in the AM and kicks off the weekend with lunch with our staff, and discussing plans for the weekend.

7:00 PM: Young families' dinner. Rabbi Mencher attends, addresses the dinner guests, and involves the children in a biblical story-telling activity during which the children color a mural depicting a variety of biblical events.

8:00 PM: At services following dinner, Rabbi Mencher addresses the congregation on the topic of "Creating a community of support and encouragement."

Saturday, January 27, 2007

9:00 AM–10:00 AM: Rabbi Mencher met and surveyed our Confirmation class, students, and their parents. Rabbi Polonsky was in attendance.

10:00 AM–1:00 PM: Shabbat morning *Chevrat Torah* services. Rabbi Mencher referred to Parashat *Bo*—the verb "*bo*" (come), used by God when sending Moses to confront Pharaoh: God did not say "*lech*" (go), teaching us that we all need someone to come with us when we confront frightening or difficult things. The entire theme of the Torah study was "building a sense of self-worth and resilience" as well as making the synagogue a place of comfort and welcome for our congregants. Lunchtime discussion followed.

Sunday, January 28, 2007

9:00 AM–10:00 AM: The Temple teaching assistants; their coordinator, Donna Robbins; and our education director, Ira Schweitzer, meet with Rabbi Mencher.

10:30 AM–12:00 PM: Our grade 5 and 6 religious school students and their parents meet Rabbi Mencher for a short introduction to the morning program, "Health, wholeness, and holiness focusing on making healthy choices in stressful situations." The students were divided into three groups for a round robin of activities consisting of communication, yoga, and nutrition.

Parents met altogether in our chapel and were presented with the same three topics but didn't move around. The yoga presentation was limited to seated breathing and visualization exercises; the nutrition presentation was all about eating a healthy breakfast. The communication component was directed at healthy communication between parent and child.

After the sessions, the parents were given evaluations to complete. Be sure to allow enough time for this. Once they left the building we never got any back, regardless of the cajoling. Parents were also given a sheet explaining KHG and what we were all about. The initial intention was to solicit donations to support the program, but one of our rabbis vetoed that part of the handout, given that the most important issue behind the whole initiative was to give to people without asking something back right away.

It was originally planned that each activity center would have a signpost containing a biblical reference in Hebrew and English. Unfortunately the signs weren't big enough to draw any attention. Suggestion: bigger signs should be used and more effort should be made to link the tradition and the offered activities so as to provide a spiritual context.

Results

The parental feedback to this session was extremely positive. They found the sessions interesting, relevant to their lives, and informative.

About eighty parents were in attendance. The only criticism was that the program was too short and that they wanted more.

The student round robin sessions were each about twenty minutes long and there were about twenty students in each session. Two of the sessions were held on opposite corners of one of our halls. This posed a problem regarding sound. One of the groups had a microphone and the other didn't. So the group communication without the microphone was the least successful. When we do this again, we'll make sure that each group has its own room and proper sound equipment.

To hear more of Temple Sinai's story, and for more information and full program details, please contact the URJ Department of Jewish Family Concerns.

Best Practices 2: Sample Program Materials from Congregation Rodef Shalom in Pittsburgh

In response to a tragic death of an area teen involved in risky behavior, congregation Rodef Shalom sought consultation with the URJ Department of Jewish Family Concerns and with the Jewish Family and Children's Service (JFCS). As a result, Rodef Shalom put together a session on Adolescent Risky Behavior, which was open to the community at large. Following that session, it became clear that students and parents were left with many more questions and requested more programming on theses issues. This is how, in a nutshell, "A Year of Adolescent Programming" came to exist.

This chapter provides some sample materials from Rodef Shalom's project and descriptions of the group sessions that took place.[2]

The Program Timetable

Adolescent Programming
Rabbi Edie Mencher, Abby Gilbert, Helene Kessler Burke
Sunday, February 11, 2007
Kids—Juggling Friends, Schools, and Parents—
Ways of Managing the Pressure!
Parents—Helping Our Kids to Make It in a Sometimes Tough World

Staffing

- Rabbi Edythe Mencher, Assistant Director URJ Family Concerns
- Abby Gilbert, URJ PA Regional Director of Youth and Informal Education
- Helene Kessler Burke, Director of Youth Education at Rodef Shalom

---

[2]Pilot programs of *Resilience of the Soul* were introduced in congregations under the project's former title, *Kedushat HaGuf*. All references to the project in this document will therefore be under the title of *Kedushat HaGuf.*

- Rabbis Aaron Bisno, Sharyn Henry, and Daniel Young—Rodef Shalom
- JFCS
- Pediatricians
- Teachers, local specialists in art, drama, writing, sports

| 9:30 AM–11:00 AM | Grades 6–8 |
| 11:00 AM–12:30 PM | Grades 9–12 |

Program Highlights

Why *Kedushat HaGuf*? To introduce the concept of resilience to your congregation. What is resilience? How is it built?
It is the idea that we can be taught how to manage life's challenges in ways that promote health and wholeness. Resilience is built when individuals have an opportunity to

- Experience themselves as worthwhile, cherished, and capable.
- Share their experiences, express their concerns, and have their feelings validated.
- Remember positive ways in which they have managed in the past.
- Discover new ways to solve problems and find calm.
- Draw upon human and spiritual sources of affirmation, cooperation, acceptance, and hope.

Schedule from the URJ *Kedushat HaGuf,* The Holiness of the Body, Brochure

| 9:30 AM–10:00 AM | Rabbi Mencher will deliver "keynote" to students and parents |
| 10:00 AM–11:00 AM | Breakout Sessions: |

Rabbi Mencher, rabbis, and JFCS (?) will conduct workshop with parents[3]
- Will be somewhat experiential—what helps you to cope, what does not.
- Remember personal feelings.
- Possible guided meditation, writing letters.

Students will choose from the following electives: All of these activities help you to manage feelings in a nondestructive way
- Sports—noncompetitive (team building, strengthens you, calms you down)
- Torah yoga
- Judaic arts—personal expressions
- Journaling, poetry
- Music

Program will repeat at 11:00 AM–12:30 PM for grades 9–12 and on Monday evening at Temple Emanuel for the South Hills community of teens.

This program was made possible through a generous contribution from the Synagogue Learning Innovation Grant Fund of the United Jewish Federation Foundation, the Agency for Jewish Learning, and the Jacob Religious School of Rodef Shalom Congregation.

---

[3]For full details of this particular activity see What Helps and What Doesn't: Ruth Versus Elkanah (page 117).

Descriptions of Group Sessions

The presenters in the sessions above were asked to write a short synopsis of what they actually did in their groups, as well as share some students responses. This is some of what they wrote:

Art Therapy: A Nondestructive Way of Self Expression
led by Dafna Rehavia-Hanauer, Art Psychotherapist, MA CAT ATR

Art Program

9:30 AM–11:00 AM First Group: Grades 6–8
11:00 AM–11:50 AM Second Group: Grades 9–12
Art Program Stations
Station 1: Painting
  • Creating free paintings using poster colors and oil pastels.
  • Materials: paper, brushes, paint, color plates, possible nature magazines for ideas.
Station 2: Craft
  • Creating necklaces from paper clips and buttons.
  • Materials: Paper clips, colored paper from journals, glue, buttons, thread.
Station 3: Puppets
  • Creating imaginary puppets.
  • Materials: empty ice cream container, glue, paper, secures, yarn, etc.
Station 4: Wood/Linoleum Carving
  • Creating an object or landscape using carving technique.
  • Materials: Linoleum, wood carving tools, rollers, flat plastic surface, water-based print color, paper.
Station 5: Etching
  • Creating a surface or using a ready surface to create an etching of your choice.
  • Materials: small hard board surfaces, colored plastelina (modeling clay), pencils (sharp tools for etching).
  • Black magic paper.
Station 6: Collage (if needed)
  • Create a collage.
  • Materials: Magazines and glue. (Magazines specifically of nature and art journals can be added to help enhance creative ideas.)

Art offers a safe and constructive way of expressing negative feelings resulting from the pressures of growing up in our society. Art can function as a replacement for the need to harm oneself and one's body. Artistic creation offers a concrete way of expressing anger while at the same time presents an opportunity through self-expression to enhance self-esteem. Artistic expression has the power to take very negative feelings and states and transform them into creative power that provides positive feedback and a sense of accomplishment. For many of us it is difficult to know exactly what the causes of our destructive behaviors are and how to treat them. It is also difficult to help our children to cope with their stress and understand the meaning of "*Kedushat HaGuf.*"

As an art therapist I am looking for artistic ways to engage children in creative activity. This workshop dealing with the concept of "*Kedushat HaGuf*" gave me the opportunity to meet with teenagers of our community through a process of artistic creation. The artistic creation at this workshop meant to open the door for an artistic, therapeutic experience.

The group of teens came into the art room and found themselves in front of a variety of creative options. I explained to the teens the importance of creative expression for them, not only as a release for hard feelings and pressure, but also as another way to communicate with others and a way to discover their own powers. I told them, "You all have the ability and talent to create! In order to discover it, all you need is the opportunity to explore it. The way to explore one's own talent and creativity is through experiencing the artistic materials, looking for what feels most right for you to explore at the moment." As the participants were finding the materials they wanted to experience, I added that they are free to play and explore the materials: "I am not going to tell you what to do, your creativity will lead you. The examples I am showing are only offers, and it is up to you to choose" (as they just chose the right materials). During the workshop I was moving from one art station to the other, engaging the teens through their emerging creation. For some I offered to explore other materials when done, as I thought therapeutically they will benefit from it. For instance, I offered one of the kids to explore etching on a soft artificial clay surface as I thought this would be a manner in which to experience the act of cutting in a sublimate way. Instead of self-harming he would use the same process to create a beautiful piece of art.

This workshop was a way to open the door for the teenagers to experience the modality of art and its benefits for healing feelings of anger and pressure that sometimes manifest through self-harming, such as self-mutilation, eating disorders, and substance abuse. For therapeutic continuing insight, the art objects can be used as a way of engaging children and adolescents in a discussion of their feelings and their understandings of themselves and the world.

Music
led by Eileen Freedman and Andrea Scheve

In the Music Group, African hand drums and other supportive rhythm instruments were utilized to form a cohesive group ensemble. At the beginning of our session, the teens were asked to check in with themselves and assess how they felt on a scale from 1–10 (1 = low energy, down, sad; 10 = very energetic, positive, happy). They were then introduced to the instruments and led through some call and response warm-up exercises to get comfortable on their drums. They were then introduced to some rhythms to play together and allowed space to improvise and "speak" using their drums.

We shared with the teens that drumming is a great tool to use for stress reduction and encouraged them to express themselves, both musically and verbally, whenever they felt they needed to do so. Many positive social behaviors were observed during the drum session, and the teens supported and encouraged each other throughout the entire process.

At the end of our time together, the teens were once again asked to rate themselves from 1–10. They were then asked to share whether their number had increased, decreased, or stayed the same when compared to the first assessment. Most increased and a few stayed the same. We explained that drumming has positive effects on mood and energy and that they could seek out more opportunities to participate in music-making following the day's events to reduce stress and to express themselves.

Noncompetitive Sports
led by Mike Salamon

I opened things up by asking everybody what the benefits of exercise were, and the students were able to come up with many benefits to exercise including getting in better shape, losing weight, a healthier heart, and stress reduction. At this point I tried to really emphasize stress reduction by sharing my own personal experiences. When I graduated college many years ago I had trouble finding work, so I was not very happy. In the evenings, though, I would go swimming, and it was amazing how much better my mood would be after I got out of the water. The point that I made was that exercise is like a drug. A healthy drug.

Next, I introduced a variety of different exercises that the students could do right in their rooms or homes. One exercise that seemed to challenge and interest some people were push ups with the legs on a stability ball. A few students seemed to want to impress their peers by their ability, and that is an exercise where the difficulty can easily be changed by moving the position on the ball. I also tried to emphasize that this type of exercise would be good for sports training since so many of the students are involved in sports (I took a poll of this at the beginning).

For the younger group, the activity that seemed to go over best was a quick obstacle course that I created, which again is something that each student could create in his or her own home. To create interest, I timed each person, though many students were quick to point out that the title of the class was "Noncompetitive Sports." I told the group that it was okay to compete with themselves for time, and in the end I also said that it wasn't important how fast they really went, but that they were keeping active and enjoying themselves.

Journaling
led by Laurie Arnold

I led journaling/writing groups. I shared ideas about how writing can offer solace, a way to learn about ourselves, and give opportunities to take risks and find out what is hoped for. Participants wrote to prompts that were drawn from poems we read together in the sessions, the themes of which revolved around resiliency. The topics that emerged from group discussions and writing were: challenging oneself, courage, fear, listening to oneself, self-criticism, dreams, survivor qualities, meaning in life, and handling difficult times.

A student remarked about the journaling process, "I can see myself actually change right there. I can see how I was and what I am now. It is for me important to see this change and know I'm not stuck." Another said, "I'm deep; I like thinking through my thoughts on paper, it helps me figure things out. Emotions are not that big a deal."

We created a group story based on the line, "My real me is most proud of . . . ," and from that the group each wrote a reaction to each others' responses further facilitating discussion about ourselves and our lives.

Writing is a strength-based, open-ended creative art that allows the process to carry the participant as far as they want to go. The sharing process helps to break down barriers and to create community. When sharing only with ourselves on the page, we hear our own voice much stronger and when we feel the need to share with others what we have written, we experience we aren't alone in our feelings, even though our feelings are unique.

The journal is a safe container for emotions. As one girl remarked, "If I can write about it, I can understand more about what's really bothering me. And that really helps sometimes. Like when I'm really mad, I can write it out instead of fighting. After writing I'm not that upset. I can think it through."

Participants wrote poignantly and freely about their dreams, and discussed where they "tucked" their dreams and what they do, or want to do, that can bring their dreams into reality. We practiced free writing and emphasized freedom from spelling constraints or grammar, so as to not limit personal expression. I emphasized that writing is an activity for not knowing what we feel or why we feel it, just as much as it is for knowing what we feel.

Yoga
led by Mickie Diamond

Three groups were offered for the Rodef Shalom teen program. At the Rodef Shalom site two groups met on a Sunday morning and were split up by age with approximately twelve teens in each group. The Temple Emanuel group met on a weeknight and combined ages to make one group of approximately sixteen teens.

The goal of the program was to offer relaxation and yoga techniques that the group could learn to use effectively when they find themselves in stressful situations. The hope was that by teaching techniques such as these, teens would be offered natural coping mechanisms that would lead to healthy alternatives to drug use and destructive behaviors.

Since this group would only be meeting once for an hour, this worker wanted to teach the groups quick and uncomplicated methods that they could remember and could perform with ease. Primarily what was taught were breathing exercises and deep relaxation. The Rodef groups were very receptive and appeared to enjoy the sessions. The Temple Emanuel group, however, became restless learning these gentle techniques and seemed to require more strenuous yoga postures to keep the group engaged. The group ended with deep relaxation.

While it appeared that both groups enjoyed the program, the training seemed to be more effective with the Rodef groups. This might be explained either because of the separation of the ages, offering the group on a Sunday instead of after a full day of school, a combination of both reasons, or something else. Having said that, it appeared that all three groups derived something beneficial from the sessions.

Sample Publicity Flier

Community Flyer

RODEF SHALOM
CONGREGATION

Teens and Pre-Teens: Juggling your Friends, Schools, and Parents Ways of Managing the Pressure!

Choose one activity and learn fun skills to help you manage your world in a positive way!
- Yoga with Mickie Diamond
- Arts and personal expressions with Dafna Rehavia Hanauer
- Journaling and written expression with Laurie Arnold
- Music—drumming with Eileen Freedman and Andrea Scheve
- Sports—noncompetitive with Mike Salamon

Parents: "Helping Our Kids to Make It in a Sometimes Tough World"

Join area parents as we learn how to
- Reduce stress
- Increase your tools for productive communication
- Promote resilience for ourselves, our teens, and our families

With the assistance of:
- Rabbi Edythe H. Mencher, LCSW, Associate Director of the URJ Dept. Jewish Family Concerns
- Abby Gilbert, Regional PA Director of Youth and Informal Education, URJ
- Area rabbis and social workers

as they help guide you through ways to remember how you have managed your feelings in positive ways and how we can share this with our teens to promote resilience!

Sunday, February 11, 2007
Rodef Shalom Congregation
4905 Fifth Avenue, Oakland
Open to all area Jewish kids in 6th–12th grades

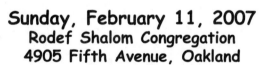

9:30 am–11:00 am: 6th–8th graders, parents, grandparents, adult friends
    9:30   Program begins in Levy Hall.
    10:00   Kids join their friends in designated areas.
    Parents will join their peers in designated area.

11:00 am–12:30 pm: 9th–12th graders, parents, grandparents, adult friends
    11:00   Program begins in Levy Hall.
    11:30   Kids join their friends in designated areas.
    Parents will join their peers in designated area.

To hear more of Congregation Rodef Shalom's story, and for more information and full program details please contact the URJ Department of Jewish Family Concerns.

Outline: Session for Parents and Synagogue Professionals on Resilience

Most important goal: Explanation of resilience and its relevance for adolescents and their families.

Most effective vehicle is: Giving powerful Jewish examples.

Core concept of program: Teens and their parents face many stresses and sometimes overwhelming emotions. It is beneficial to everyone to have some help managing without resorting to harmful choices.

What To Do

☐ Begin by talking about some of the stresses and emotions. Examples are listed below:
- **For kids:** concerns about academic, athletic, and social success; college admission; confusion about sexuality; fears about independence, leaving home; first romantic relationships or difficulty finding them; worries about meeting parents' expectations and fears of disappointing them; managing anger and fear of rejection in conflicts with family and with peers; and many more.
- **For parents:** concern about kids' academic, athletic, and social success; worries about their children making dangerous choices; concerns about whether kids will have what it takes to make it in college and the world; feelings of helplessness to protect kids; feelings of being left behind, rejected by their kids; worries about their own successes, health, relationships; their future as empty nesters; and many more.

You can elicit both parents' and kids' concerns from the group.

☐ Continue by teaching about resilience (see "What is Resilience?" on page 17))
- Tell participants what resilience is: The ability to bounce back from adversity with optimism, trust in self and others, and a sense of hope intact.
- Tell participants what we know about what helps people to be resilient, giving ancient Jewish examples and examples from contemporary Jewish life, such as those that follow. In each instance, Moses is used as an ancient example.

○ **Experience oneself as worthwhile, cherished, and capable.** Moses feels worthwhile and cherished because his parents tried so hard to save him, and they gave him a model of resourcefulness and faith by putting him in the basket in the Nile; because Pharaoh's daughter saved and adopted him; because he was raised as a prince; and because God speaks to him and trusts him with an important job.

Give contemporary examples of what makes our children feel cherished and capable and how easy it is for teenagers and parents to feel anything but cherished and capable.

○ **Having opportunities to share one's experiences, to express one's concerns, and have one's feelings validated.**

God listens and validates Moses's feelings. God does not disagree or criticize Moses's concerns when Moses says he fears he cannot confront Pharaoh because of his speech defect. God does not just tell him he speaks fine or that he can do it anyway. God promised to *lavo* (*bo*), to come, with Moses and also to send Aaron to help.

Give contemporary examples of kids expressing concerns and adults responding to the concerns. For example, a fifth-grade boy saying he will never be able to do middle school math. His parents don't negate his fear by telling him that he will be great if he tries, and that he is like his grandmother, someone who looks for things to worry about. Instead, they tell him that they understand how worried he is that he will not be ready for all of the things ahead, that he feels he might not have what it takes, and it all seems kind of overwhelming. They then move on to helping him to find solutions and think more realistically. This is usually a long discussion, and it helps to give multiple examples of various levels of seriousness. For example, finding a way to validate the girl who says everyone thinks she is ugly without agreeing with her or to validate the boy who is saying his father is unfair, dumb, and mean. It is important to stress that validating a feeling helps a kid to be clearer about what he or she is feeling and that it is understood and okay. This will help him or her to know his or her feelings, tolerate them, and then look for solutions when they are on their own.

○ **Being able to remember or being helped to remember positive ways in which they have managed in the past.**

Moses is discouraged about leading the people through the wilderness but remembers succeeding against Pharaoh with God's help.

Contemporary examples include the following: reminding a fifth grader who worries about the difficulty of learning math that he never thought he could learn to read, but succeeded at that; a girl being helped to remember how she felt like all of the other children in nursery school wouldn't like her and how she made so many friends; a boy who thinks his father is acting unfairly, remembers how he resolved things in the past when he thought his dad was unreasonable; helping a parent who worries about getting her child through high school to remember that she never thought he would separate from her in nursery school, etc.

○ **Equally helpful is having opportunities to discover new ways to solve problems and find calm.**

Jethro helped Moses to be less overwhelmed by encouraging him to appoint elders to help him legislate the Israelites.

Contemporary examples could include how we and our kids can seek help from professionals. (Have referral resources available to give out if possible.) Our children can also learn new ways of expressing feelings and calming themselves, and of taking better care of themselves in order to strengthen themselves and make themselves less vulnerable. There are many ways to achieve each of these goals with a Jewish perspective. These can include yoga, meditation, nutrition, and healthy sleep habit workshops; prayer as a way of re-finding hope and calm; Jewish journaling; noncompetitive sports; drumming and other expressive music opportunities; nature challenges; and healthy exercise. Try to have sample workshops of these available to kids and parents on the day of your program and in the weeks and months that follow.

- ○ **Be able to draw upon human and spiritual sources of affirmation, cooperation, acceptance, and hope (being able to locate one's own experiences in a context that give them meaning).**

  Moses sees his life as fitting into God's plan and his struggles as a way of bringing the Jewish people closer to the Promised Land. He sees God as experiencing some of the same disappointments and frustrations with the Israelites as he does, but it is all worth it.

  We can help our kids and their parents to see that their struggles are mirrored in Jewish tradition and history and that others have faced similar things before them, yet their lives have a purpose. For Jews, that purpose includes bringing more love and holiness into the world. Of course, this is the place to add many ideas of your own about how your congregation can help with all of these building blocks to greater resilience.

❑ If there is time, discuss harmful ways that people sometimes use to deal with stress and overwhelming emotions. It would be great to have a mental health professional join you for this discussion. (See "Coping in Ways that Hurt Us" on page 27.)

- Explain the seeming paradox that people sometimes do things that ultimately are harmful to them and that do little to actually solve their problems. These actions serve as a way of easing pain or trying to manage difficult emotional states.

- Give examples from "normal" life, such as eating too much, drinking too much, or shopping too much when we are upset about something. These actions can provide temporary relief but the overindulgence can leave us ultimately upset.

- Give examples of self-harming behaviors in which endorphins may be released and addictive patterns of pleasure from harmful behaviors established. This includes self-inflicted violence like cutting, hitting and burning, binge eating, binge drinking, extreme risk taking (high-speed driving, hanging onto moving buses, etc.), and risky masturbation practices that involve partial asphyxia.

- Give examples of how some behaviors may also serve to ease feelings of being numb and cut off from feelings (cutting may do this), give external expression of inner pain, or serve as punishment for guilt or as a reenactment of past trauma.

- Speak of how often young people can neither name the exact feeling they are experiencing nor know how to properly seek relief. They need assistance in identifying feelings, finding human support, and learning nonharmful ways to express themselves and gain relief.

- Provide participants with some important information about what to do if they suspect or know someone close to them is involved in these behaviors. Provide information on how to empathize with their distress rather than express horror at the self-destructive behavior; how to get help, but without believing the person can give up the behaviors until other more safe and effective means of achieving calm and expression are found.

- Explain that self-harming is usually not a suicidal gesture, yet those who engage in it are more likely to later make suicide attempts if the problems—depression, impulsivity, and difficulty tolerating and gaining relief from powerful feelings—are not addressed. Stress what to do to prevent suicide and how to notice warning signs of depression. (For more information consult "Suicide Prevention" on page 35.)
- Give a Jewish context to the topic:
  - *Pikuach nefesh*, our obligation to save every life.
  - *B'tzelem Elohim*, we are all made in the image of God and are here for a reason. Every one of use is deserving of care and has a mission to fulfill.
  - *Al taamod al dam re'echa*, do not stand idly by as your neighbor bleeds.
- ❏ Conclusion: Encourage participants to feel good about addressing these issues. They are already people who seek solutions and who have optimism and competence. Offer a vision of how the congregation can be a place where all members are made stronger and more resilient.

Educate Yourself

The *Kavanah* Before a Staff Meeting

When engaging the staff in an educational process related to adolescents in which self-destructive behaviors may be involved, there are some important points to keep in mind:

- There are aspects of the discussion that can make people uncomfortable, such as the mention of self-inflicted violence or correlations between adult behavior and adolescent stress. It is important to convey a sense of acceptance and understanding of how common these problems are, and to react empathically toward adults (who always want the best for kids and are afraid of feeling responsible for problems young people may develop). It is crucial to communicate that it is possible to talk about adolescent issues in a matter-of-fact way, in a nonjudgmental, accepting environment where everyone's voice is heard.

- In the discussion, make sure to stress building resilience rather than problematic behaviors. The point of educating staff about self-destructive behaviors is not to raise the anxiety level in your congregation, but rather to better equip staff to deal with these issues, and help them guide teens toward positive ways of coping with emotional turmoil.

- Resilience can be taught. Our job is to find the opportunities to build strengths and validate each child's unique experience and needs.

- Blaming parents or synagogue professionals for the pressures kids live with is counterproductive. Making people feel guilty and responsible is far less useful than offering alternatives and conveying that none of us would ever choose to damage kids through pressuring them.

- Staff may feel worried about having to cure problems. A clear message needs to be conveyed that empathy and openness is what our staff can provide. Therapy and expert advice are the realm of professionals.

- Yes, resilience *can* be taught. The very way staff speaks to kids—either the ones who are overtly hurting or the ones who may appear tough and even unkind—can make an enormous difference. The key is accepting kids and their emotions unconditionally, while offering alternatives to behavior or words that are wounding to oneself and/or others. Results may not be evident overnight, but over time, kids internalize and remember the synagogue as a place where they are cherished with all of their frailties.

- The synagogue is exactly the right setting to offer this kind of support to teens and their families. Moreover, it is a place where we can all have our sense of self-worth affirmed, our trust and faith strengthened, and where our confidence in ourselves and in others can increase.

- It is equally important to strive to make your congregation a sacred space for staff. They need to feel accepted, valued, and cared for in order to be able to support and assist members of the congregation.

Surveys for Teens, Staff, and Parents

Introduction

The information gleaned from the surveys provided here can be helpful to you in a number of ways. It can be used to help prepare programming, lesson plans, and sermons, or to understand membership trends.

For example, if the survey reveals that people are most concerned about their marriages and their children's health, you may want to ask yourself: Are these topics often addressed in the synagogue's adult-ed programs, prayer services, and sermons? If not, in what ways might you begin to integrate them?

Keep in mind that in order for people to be involved in synagogue life, they need to feel that the major issues in their lives are addressed. This does not mean the synagogue will provide solutions to everyone's problems. It does mean that it is often helpful simply to look at and reflect upon certain aspects of one's life.

Consider the following question that appears in the surveys: "Would you like there to be opportunities in synagogue for adults and teens to discuss the pressures they feel?" Sometimes, it may not even occur to people to bring their concerns to the synagogue, but it does not mean that posing the question has any less value.

How NOT to use these surveys: These surveys should not be used to raise anxiety or to evaluate performance of parents and/or staff. In other words, these are not scientific tools and should not be used as such. No synagogue president should confront the educator with this; no parent should be made to feel inadequate over what teens have revealed. This would constitute a misuse of these surveys. People rarely get an opportunity to be this candid. It would be wise to remember this, and use these surveys accordingly.

It is far more useful to view these surveys as icebreakers and as stimuli for thought and discussion than as statistically valid. Thus, they should be presented as ways for the synagogue and the Reform Movement to gather information on how to be most helpful for our members. Finally, remember that this is merely a tool. As such, you can choose to use it or not, and you are encouraged to adapt and change it to suit your own needs.

Teen Survey

This survey is designed to elicit your knowledge and personal experience with stress as a young person. Our goal is to gain greater understanding of the stresses and pressures in the lives of teens and young adults so that clergy, educators, congregations, camps, youth groups, and lay leaders can work together to be certain our Jewish communities respond to the real needs of the young people and families.

There is no need to identify yourself on this questionnaire. We are seeking to learn about the issues that you see as most pressing in the lives of young people. We want to know how young people seek to manage these issues and to ascertain what information and programs would be most helpful, as well as what changes in the way parents; clergy; congregational, camp, and youth group leaders respond would be most helpful.

1. Please rate on a scale of 1–5 each of these issues as to how much of a subject of concern and source of pressure you think they are for you? Please use the following scale and circle your degree of concern.

  1 No concern
  2 A Little Concern
  3 Some Concern
  4 Considerable Concern
  5 Most Concern

Academic achievement	1	2	3	4	5
Worries about disappointing your parents	1	2	3	4	5
Feeling like you are not a good person	1	2	3	4	5
Appearance: weight, complexion, height, puberty-related concerns	1	2	3	4	5
Athletic achievement	1	2	3	4	5
Popularity with peers (fitting in, being accepted)	1	2	3	4	5
Making appropriate choices about sexual involvement	1	2	3	4	5
Sexual orientation	1	2	3	4	5
Using drugs, including marijuana and alcohol	1	2	3	4	5
Pregnancy and related issues	1	2	3	4	5
Sexually transmitted diseases	1	2	3	4	5
Concerns about your health or survival	1	2	3	4	5

Anxiety about the world situation	1	2	3	4	5
Moodiness	1	2	3	4	5
Conflicts with parents and/or other family members	1	2	3	4	5
Worries about status	1	2	3	4	5
Loneliness and feeling different	1	2	3	4	5
Health of family members	1	2	3	4	5
Public speaking and performance	1	2	3	4	5
Concerns about God, religion	1	2	3	4	5
Concerns about whether anyone is watching over us	1	2	3	4	5
Worries about having what it takes to become independent	1	2	3	4	5
Worries about losing friends	1	2	3	4	5
Worries about money	1	2	3	4	5
Difficulties in romantic relationships	1	2	3	4	5
Worries about managing your temper	1	2	3	4	5
Parents' marital conflicts and/or divorce	1	2	3	4	5

2. When you are worried, angry, feeling guilty, frightened, confused, or even depressed, which of the following might you or teens you know do to deal with these feelings?

a. Talk about the situation with friends	Never	Sometimes	Frequently
b. Talk about the situation with a parent	Never	Sometimes	Frequently
c. Talk about the situation with a family member other than a parent	Never	Sometimes	Frequently
d. Talk about the situation with a member of the clergy	Never	Sometimes	Frequently
e. Talk about the situation with a youth group leader or camp counselor	Never	Sometimes	Frequently
f. Talk about the situation with a guidance counselor or teacher	Never	Sometimes	Frequently
g. Talk about the situation with a therapist	Never	Sometimes	Frequently

		Never	Sometimes	Frequently
h.	Pray	Never	Sometimes	Frequently
i.	Listen to music, sing	Never	Sometimes	Frequently
j.	Read a book to distract yourself	Never	Sometimes	Frequently
k.	Find information to manage your problem	Never	Sometimes	Frequently
l.	Meditate, do yoga	Never	Sometimes	Frequently
m.	Exercise, play sports	Never	Sometimes	Frequently
n.	Go shopping	Never	Sometimes	Frequently
o.	Eat foods you enjoy in moderation	Never	Sometimes	Frequently
p.	Drink alcohol	Never	Sometimes	Frequently
q.	Use drugs	Never	Sometimes	Frequently
r.	Write down your feelings	Never	Sometimes	Frequently
s.	Go online to chat rooms	Never	Sometimes	Frequently
t.	Watch TV or movies	Never	Sometimes	Frequently
u.	Go on an eating binge	Never	Sometimes	Frequently
v.	Cut, burn, or hurt yourself in some way	Never	Sometimes	Frequently
w.	Deprive yourself of food	Never	Sometimes	Frequently
x.	Deprive yourself of some favorite activity	Never	Sometimes	Frequently
y.	Do deep breathing exercises	Never	Sometimes	Frequently
z.	Shoplift or partake in other risky and/or illegal but sometimes thrilling behavior	Never	Sometimes	Frequently

3. Please list/describe any other issues that you are concerned about and/or that you know concern other young people. If you need more space, you can continue on the back.

_____

_____

4. Have you yourself ever felt sad and hopeless for more than a few days? Or do you know someone who has? Please elaborate.

_____

_____

5. Do you believe a few, some, many, or most kids get depressed?

        Few   Some   Many   Most

6. Do you know anyone who has expressed suicidal ideas?

        Yes   No

7. Would you know what to do if you had concerns about your own depression or some-one else's?

　　　　　Yes　　　　　No

8. Have you yourself experienced or do you know kids who have a problem related to eating like anorexia, bulimia, or frequent overeating or under eating?

　　　　　Yes　　　　No

　If yes, how many kids have such problems (in your opinion)

　　　　Few　　　　　Some　　　　　Many　　　　　Most

9. Circle what you have found to be the most helpful sources of information on the sub-jects of teen problems like depression, eating disorders, peer pressure, etc.

　Internet　　TV Shows　　　Friends　　Movies　　　Books　　　Parents

　School Programs　　　Camp Programs　　　Synagogue Programs

10. Would you like your parents to know more about the issues that concern teens?

　　　　　Yes　　No

11. If you could give parents one message about how to help their kids, what would it be?

　_____

　_____

12. Would you like to have opportunities in camp to discuss the pressures kids feel?

　_____

　_____

13. Would you like to have opportunities in camp to discover better ways of reducing stress and maintaining health and balance? Please elaborate.

　_____

　_____

14. Would you like to have opportunities to discuss pressures and to discover ways of reducing stress in Youth Group? Please elaborate.

　_____

　_____

15. Would you like to have the clergy and educators in your home congregation offer opportunities for kids and parents to learn more about the pressures kids experience? Please elaborate.

　_____

　_____

16. Are there ways in which your Judaism helps you to manage the difficult choices and feelings that are part of your life? Please elaborate.

_____

_____

17. If you could give the staff at camp one message about teen pressures, what would that be?

_____

_____

Staff Survey

This survey is designed to elicit your knowledge and experience on what you believe are the sources of stress experienced by young people.

There is no need to identify yourself on this questionnaire.

In the long term, this survey will help your congregation assess and evaluate the experience of synagogue staff concerning the issues raised in *Resilience of the Soul* so that an optimal program to build adolescent resilience can be implemented—one uniquely suited to the needs of the congregation.

We at the Department of Jewish Family Concerns will appreciate your forwarding results to us so that we can we can get a clear picture of what the needs, interests, and opinions are at various congregations. We will share that information (but protect confidentiality) with other congregations so we can all benefit from each other's wisdom and experience.

1. Please rate on a scale of 1–5 each of these issues as to how much of a subject of concern and source of pressure you think they are for young people? Please use the following scale and circle your degree of concern.

    1 No concern
    2 A Little Concern
    3 Some Concern
    4 Considerable Concern
    5 Most Concern

Academic achievement	1	2	3	4	5
Worries about disappointing their parents	1	2	3	4	5
Feeling like they are not a good person	1	2	3	4	5
Appearance: weight, complexion, height, puberty-related concerns	1	2	3	4	5
Athletic achievement	1	2	3	4	5
Popularity with peers (fitting in, being accepted)	1	2	3	4	5

Making appropriate choices about sexual involvement	1	2	3	4	5
Sexual orientation	1	2	3	4	5
Using drugs, including marijuana and alcohol	1	2	3	4	5
Pregnancy and related issues	1	2	3	4	5
Sexually transmitted diseases	1	2	3	4	5
Concerns about their health or survival	1	2	3	4	5
Anxiety about the world situation	1	2	3	4	5
Moodiness	1	2	3	4	5
Conflicts with parents and/or other family members	1	2	3	4	5
Worries about status (financial, social)	1	2	3	4	5
Loneliness and feeling different	1	2	3	4	5
Health of family members	1	2	3	4	5
Public speaking and performance	1	2	3	4	5
Concerns about God, religion	1	2	3	4	5
Concerns about whether anyone is watching over them	1	2	3	4	5
Worries about having what it takes to become independent	1	2	3	4	5
Worries about losing friends	1	2	3	4	5
Worries about money	1	2	3	4	5
Difficulties in romantic relationships	1	2	3	4	5
Worries about managing their temper	1	2	3	4	5
Parents' marital conflicts and/or divorce	1	2	3	4	5

2. When teens/young adults are worried, angry, feeling guilty, frightened, confused or even depressed, which of the following, in your opinion, might they do to deal with these feelings?

   a. Talk about the situation with friends   Never   Sometimes   Frequently

b.	Talk about the situation with a parent	Never	Sometimes	Frequently
c.	Talk about the situation with a family member other than a parent	Never	Sometimes	Frequently
d.	Talk about the situation with a member of the clergy	Never	Sometimes	Frequently
e.	Talk about the situation with a youth group leader or camp counselor	Never	Sometimes	Frequently
f.	Talk about the situation with a guidance counselor or teacher	Never	Sometimes	Frequently
g.	Talk about the situation with a therapist	Never	Sometimes	Frequently
h.	Pray	Never	Sometimes	Frequently
i.	Listen to music, sing	Never	Sometimes	Frequently
j.	Read a book to distract themselves	Never	Sometimes	Frequently
k.	Find information to manage their problem	Never	Sometimes	Frequently
l.	Meditate, do yoga	Never	Sometimes	Frequently
m.	Exercise, play sports	Never	Sometimes	Frequently
n.	Go shopping	Never	Sometimes	Frequently
o.	Eat foods they enjoy in moderation	Never	Sometimes	Frequently
p.	Drink alcohol	Never	Sometimes	Frequently
q.	Use drugs	Never	Sometimes	Frequently
r.	Write down their feelings	Never	Sometimes	Frequently
s.	Go online to chat rooms	Never	Sometimes	Frequently
t.	Watch TV or movies	Never	Sometimes	Frequently
u.	Go on an eating binge	Never	Sometimes	Frequently
v.	Cut, burn, or hurt themselves some way	Never	Sometimes	Frequently
w.	Deprive themselves of food	Never	Sometimes	Frequently
x.	Deprive themselves of some favorite activity	Never	Sometimes	Frequently
y.	Do deep breathing exercises	Never	Sometimes	Frequently
z.	Shoplift or partake in other risky and/or illegal but sometimes thrilling behavior	Never	Sometimes	Frequently

3. Please list/describe any other venues/solutions that you think young people might seek to manage difficult feelings.

_____

_____

4. Do you believe a few, some, many, or most teens get depressed? Circle what you think is the frequency of depression among young adults.

    Few   Some   Many   Most

    Please provide an estimate as to **how many or what percentage** of teens you believe feel/felt this way: _____

    To the best of your knowledge, do other members of the staff share this belief?

    Yes   No   Don't know

5. Do you know a teen or teens who has expressed suicidal ideas?

    Yes   No

    If yes, how many? _____.

    To the best of your knowledge, are other members of the staff aware of this?

    Yes   No   Don't know

6. Would you know what to do if you had concerns regarding a teen who is exhibiting signs of depression?

    Yes   No

7. Have you personally, in your work with teens, come across or heard of teens who have a problem related to eating like anorexia, bulimia, frequent overeating or under eating?

    Yes   No

    If yes, how many kids in your opinion have such problems?

    Few   Some   Many   Most

    To the best of your knowledge, are other members of the staff aware of this?

    Yes   No   Don't know

8. Would you know what to do if you had concerns regarding a teen who is exhibiting signs of having an eating disorder?

    Yes   No

9. Have you personally, in your work with teens, come across someone who cuts, burns, or hurts him- or herself in any way?

    Yes   No

    If yes, how many? _____.

    To the best of your knowledge, are other members of the staff aware of this?

    Yes   No   Don't know

10. Would you know what to do if you had concerns regarding a teen who engages in self-destructive behavior?

                Yes   No

11. Circle what you believe to be the most helpful sources of information for teens on the subjects of teen problems like depression, eating disorders, peer pressure, etc.

    Internet   TV Shows   Friends   Movies
    Books   Parents   School Programs   Camp Programs
    Synagogue Programs

12. Do you believe parents need to know more about the issues that concern teens?

                Yes   No

13. If you could give parents one message about how to help their kids, what would it be?

    _____

    _____

14. Would you like there to be opportunities in synagogue/religious school/youth group/camp for teens to discuss the pressures they feel? In your response, please list the venues where you think such opportunities should exist.

    _____

    _____

15. Would you like there to be opportunities in synagogue/religious school/youth group/camp for teens to discover better ways of reducing stress and maintaining health and balance? In your response, please list the venues where you think such opportunities should exist.

    _____

    _____

16. Do you feel supported by your synagogue/camp/youth group leadership/ administration, etc., in terms of them providing resources, knowledge, and counseling so that you can be best positioned to respond to challenges presented by young people? Please elaborate.

    _____

    _____

17. Would you like to have opportunities to discuss your own concerns, as a staff member, on this issue? Please elaborate.

    _____

    _____

18. In what areas would you as a staff member like to receive more information or train-ing so as to respond to teen concerns and needs in the most constructive way?

   _____

   _____

19. In your opinion, does Judaism potentially offer ways to help kids manage the difficult choices and feelings that are part of their life? Please elaborate.

   _____

   _____

20. If you could give the young people you work with one message about pressures and how to manage them, what would that be?

   _____

   _____

Parent Survey

This survey is designed to generate your knowledge and experiences on what you believe are sources of stress and help.
   There is no need to identify yourself on this questionnaire.
   In the long term, the survey will help your congregation and the Reform Movement to evaluate the issues and suggestions raised in *Resilience of the Soul*. Our goal is to understand adolescent and adult concerns and to create congregational responses that will build emo-tional and spiritual resiliency.
   We at the Department of Jewish Family Concerns will appreciate your forwarding results to us so that we can get a clear picture of what the needs, interests, and opinions are at various congregations. We will share that information (but strictly protect confi-dentiality) with other congregations so we can all benefit from each other's wisdom and experience.

1. Please rate on a scale of 1–5 each of these issues as to how much of a subject of con-cern and source of pressure you think they are for you? Please use the following scale and circle your degree of concern.

       1 No concern
       2 A Little Concern
       3 Some Concern
       4 Considerable Concern
       5 Most Concern

Professional achievement	1	2	3	4	5
Professional satisfaction	1	2	3	4	5
Worries about marriage or relationship to romantic partner	1	2	3	4	5

Concerns about children's health	1	2	3	4	5
Concerns about children's appearance, weight, physique	1	2	3	4	5
Concerns about children's academic performance	1	2	3	4	5
Concerns about children's popularity, social acceptance	1	2	3	4	5
Own appearance, weight, signs of aging, physique	1	2	3	4	5
Athletic achievement and fitness	1	2	3	4	5
Social life and status among peers (fitting in, being accepted)	1	2	3	4	5
Making sound sexual choices	1	2	3	4	5
Sexual orientation	1	2	3	4	5
Children using drugs, including marijuana and alcohol	1	2	3	4	5
Children's sexuality and sexual choices	1	2	3	4	5
Concerns about your own health or survival	1	2	3	4	5
Anxiety about the world situation	1	2	3	4	5
Conflicts with children and/or other family members	1	2	3	4	5
Worries about aging parents	1	2	3	4	5
Worries about financial status	1	2	3	4	5
Loneliness and feeling different	1	2	3	4	5
Health of family members	1	2	3	4	5
Public speaking and performance	1	2	3	4	5
Concerns about God, religion	1	2	3	4	5
Concerns about whether anyone is watching over us	1	2	3	4	5
Worries about having what it takes to live independently (concerns about empty nest; possibility of remaining or becoming single via divorce or death of your spouse)	1	2	3	4	5

Worries about losing friends	1	2	3	4	5
Worries about money	1	2	3	4	5
Difficulty with romantic relationships	1	2	3	4	5
Worries about managing your temper	1	2	3	4	5
Worries about mortality	1	2	3	4	5

2. When you are worried, angry, feeling guilty, frightened, confused, or even depressed, which of the following do you participate in to deal with these feelings?

a. Talk about the situation with friends	Never	Sometimes	Frequently
b. Talk about the situation with a spouse or partner	Never	Sometimes	Frequently
c. Talk about the situation with a family member other than a spouse or partner	Never	Sometimes	Frequently
d. Talk about the situation with member of the clergy	Never	Sometimes	Frequently
e. Talk about the situation with a professional advisor or mentor	Never	Sometimes	Frequently
f. Talk about the situation with a therapist	Never	Sometimes	Frequently
g. Pray	Never	Sometimes	Frequently
h. Listen to music, sing	Never	Sometimes	Frequently
i. Read a book to distract yourself	Never	Sometimes	Frequently
j. Find information to manage your problem	Never	Sometimes	Frequently
k. Meditate, do yoga	Never	Sometimes	Frequently
l. Exercise, play sports	Never	Sometimes	Frequently
m. Go shopping	Never	Sometimes	Frequently
n. Eat foods you enjoy in moderation	Never	Sometimes	Frequently
o. Seek sexual relations	Never	Sometimes	Frequently
p. Drink alcohol	Never	Sometimes	Frequently
q. Use drugs	Never	Sometimes	Frequently
r. Write down your feelings	Never	Sometimes	Frequently
s. Go online to chat rooms	Never	Sometimes	Frequently
t. Watch TV or movies	Never	Sometimes	Frequently
u. Go on an eating binge	Never	Sometimes	Frequently

v. Cut, burn, or hurt yourself in some way	Never	Sometimes	Frequently
w. Deprive yourself of food	Never	Sometimes	Frequently
x. Deprive yourself of some favorite activity	Never	Sometimes	Frequently
y. Do deep breathing exercises	Never	Sometimes	Frequently
z. Shoplift, gamble, or partake in other risky and/or illegal but sometimes thrilling behavior	Never	Sometimes	Frequently

3. Please list/describe any other venues/solutions that you think adults might seek to manage difficult feelings.

_____

_____

4. Do you believe adults get depressed?

    Yes   No

If yes, circle what you think is the frequency of depression among adults:

    Few   Some   Many   Most

Please provide an estimate as to what percentage of adults you believe have been depressed: _____

To the best of your knowledge, do other members of the community share this belief?

    Yes   No   Don't know/Maybe

5. Do you know an adult who has expressed suicidal ideas?

    Yes   No

If yes, how many? _____

To the best of your knowledge, are members of the synagogue staff likely to be aware of serious depression among congregants?

    Yes   No   Don't know/Maybe

6. Do you believe teens get depressed?

    Yes   No

Please provide an estimate as to **how many or what percentage** of teens you believe have been depressed: _____

To the best of your knowledge, do other members of the community share this belief?

    Yes   No   Don't know/Maybe

7. Do you know any teens who have expressed suicidal ideas?

    Yes   No

If yes, how many? _____

To the best of your knowledge, are members of the synagogue staff likely to be aware of serious depression among teens?

       Yes   No   Don't know/Maybe

8. Would you know what to do if you had concerns regarding an adult or teen who is exhibiting signs of depression?

       Yes   No

9. Have you, someone in your family, or someone in your close circle of friends had a problem related to eating like anorexia, bulimia, or frequent overeating or under eating?

       Yes   No

If yes, how many other families do you think are dealing with such problems?

       Few   Some   Many   Most

To the best of your knowledge, are other members of the synagogue staff aware of this?

       Yes   No   Don't know/Maybe

10. Would you know what to do if you had concerns regarding another adult or teen who is exhibiting signs of having an eating disorder?

       Yes   No

11. Have you personally come across someone who purposefully cuts, burns, or hurts him- or herself in any way?

       Yes   No

If yes, how many? _____

To the best of your knowledge, are professionals at the synagogue aware of these behaviors?

       Yes   No   Don't know/Maybe

12. Would you know what to do if you had concerns regarding a teen or an adult who engages in self-destructive behavior?

       Yes   No

13. Circle what you believe to be the most helpful sources of information on the subjects of adult/teen problems like depression, eating disorders, peer pressure, etc.

Internet	TV Shows	Friends	Movies
Parents	School Programs	Magazines	Camp Programs
Synagogue Programs	Therapist		

14. Do you believe congregants and family members need to know more about the issues that concern adults and teens in their community and in their families?

       Yes   No

15. If you could give the staff of the congregation one message about how to be more helpful to adults and teens what would it be?

_____

_____

16. Would you like there to be opportunities in synagogue for adults and teens to discuss the pressures they feel? Please elaborate.

_____

_____

17. Would you like there to be opportunities in synagogue for teens and adults to discover better ways of reducing stress and maintaining health and balance? Please elaborate.

_____

_____

18. Do you feel supported by your congregation in terms of the availability of resources, knowledge, and counseling so that you can be best positioned to respond to challenges in your own life and in the life of your teen? Please elaborate.

_____

_____

19. Would you like to have opportunities to discuss your own concerns, as a parent, on this issue? Please elaborate.

_____

_____

20. In what areas would you, as an adult congregant and parent, like to receive more information or training so as to know how to respond constructively to adult and teen concerns/needs from a Jewish perspective?

_____

_____

21. In your opinion, does Judaism potentially offer ways to help us manage the difficult choices and feelings that are part of our lives? Please elaborate.

_____

_____

22. If you could give the adults and young people in your life one message about pressures and how to manage them, what would that be?

_____

_____

Section 5

Program Ideas, Exercises, and Suggestions

How We Eat

A Healthy Approach to Nutrition Inspired by Jewish Wisdom

This is a Jewish resource on healthy nutrition. The information presented here can serve as the basis for a parent-child meeting, can be adapted into a handout, or developed into a sermon. For example, planning a congregational evening with a nutritionist can be a good way to teach teens about the importance of self-nurturing and how we can draw sustenance in treating our bodies well.

גֹּמֵל נַפְשׁוֹ אִישׁ חָסֶד

"He who does good to his own person is a man of mercy" (Proverbs 11:17).

In Judaism, nurturing oneself is not only encouraged and necessary, but is considered an act of great benevolence. Eating, the most obvious act of nurturing the self, can become an act of great kindness. It can be a way of reminding ourselves that in order to love and be loved, we must first let our own bodies feel loved, nurtured, and cherished. Feeding ourselves ought to be a way for us to show love for ourselves; to establish that we are precious and worthy of care. Food is a great source of pleasure, and Judaism always encourages us to take pleasure and to enjoy life.

The way in which we are fed by the people who love us shows us we are loved, and teaches us how to love ourselves. The way in which we regard food is worth paying attention to, because it can teach us how we really feel about ourselves in areas that we may not be accustomed to thinking about. Do we regard food negatively? Do we use disparaging labels to describe food, such as "bad" and "junk"? Do we regard our bodies in a negative manner, calling them "fat," "ugly," or "gross"?

Naturally, some foods are healthier than others, and some bodies more fit than others. The issue is complex, but the main lesson to be learned is how to make a distinction between damaging oneself with caustic self-criticism and nurturing oneself with beneficial self-care.

For many people, food is a way to cope with all types of hungers and desires, not all physical. *Ta'ava*, the Hebrew word for "lust," means having a strong desire to possess or acquire something that we do not really need. *Ta'ava* can clearly be negative as in cases when people lust uncontrollably after power, fame, and money. At its core, however, the drive, the yearning can be positive. In the Book of Isaiah we learn about yearning for God:

לְשִׁמְךָ וּלְזִכְרְךָ תַּאֲוַת־נָפֶשׁ: נַפְשִׁי אִוִּיתִיךָ בַּלַּיְלָה

"We long for the name by which you are called. At night I yearn for you with all my being" (Isaiah 26:8–9).

Having *ta'ava*, as every human being has, is a learning opportunity. It is a way for us to come to terms with our hungers, desires, wants, and needs; it is a way to learn how to fulfill them without overfilling ourselves, and in the process to better know who we are.

It is crucial that we learn and teach how to develop healthy ways to care for our own selves without harming ourselves or others. This means that we must pay attention to how we eat. Children form eating habits at an early age. Just like parents feed their children, when the people Israel were in the desert, they were fed the magical manna by God. We read that they were not only given physical sustenance, but were also taught the skill of how to eat:

"At first Israel were like hens randomly pecking away in a heap of refuse, until Moses came and fixed definite mealtimes for them" (Bavli Yoma 75b).

Moses taught the Israelites. Children need to learn from their parents about the importance of regular, wholesome meals.

Mealtime Tips[1]

- **Plan meals around the four food groups**: (1) Grains, (2) Meat and alternatives, (3) Vegetables and Fruit, and (4) Milk Products.
- **Cook your meals together** so that you can spend time together as a family and everybody can learn from each other about healthy food.
- **Make sure your teens know how to read food labels.** Soon they'll be choosing healthier options for themselves.
- **Maintain a variety of foods in your home.** Over time your teens will be willing to try new foods.
- **Be a good role model** by practicing healthy eating habits at home and at restaurants.
- **Turn the TV off** so everyone can enjoy eating together.
- Visit **www.heartandstroke.ca** and **www.healthcheck.org** for more information on healthy living and great recipes.

"The stomach carries the legs" (B'reishit Rabbah 70:8).

Doctors and nutritionists remind us that we need to teach our children how to find the right balance between the energy they take from food and drink and the energy they use to grow and be active. As for adults, eating a balanced diet (energy in) and exercising regularly (energy out), will make one feel healthier, and chances are when one feels better, so will one's children.

---

[1]Nutritional and health information taken from Heart and Stroke Foundation of Canada, "Healthy Eating Choices for Your Children," *Health Check*, **www.healthcheck.org**.

"By toil shall you eat of it" (Genesis 3:17).

In the Garden of Eden, Adam and Eve were given nourishment without having to toil for it. After the banishment, that was no longer the case. We do have to toil for our food—in the obvious sense of having to work to put food on the table, and in the not-so-obvious sense of having to invest thought, effort, and planning into what we put into our bodies. It is not always easy to plan what we eat in advance. But last-minute meals, as we all know, can be very stressful, as well as not sufficiently nourishing. The "toil" is worth it. Meal planning is one of the most important steps to enjoying nutritious meals every day.

Meal Planning Tips

- **Keep a shopping list in the kitchen.** Visit **www.healthcheck.org** for a printable list.
- **Set aside one day when you can write down your week's meal plan.** Plan your meals and snacks around the four food groups and make sure to include enough food to meet everyone's nutritional needs.
- **Plan for quick meals** for those nights when there are after-school or evening activities.
- **Let teenagers make one meal a week.** They are more likely to eat what they have helped to prepare. Suggest ideas such as soups, sandwiches, simple casseroles, or pizzas made with pita and their favorite toppings.
- **Consider planning two to three weeks** of menus that you can repeat.
- **Make an extra batch** of your favorite soup or pasta for the freezer so you can defrost, heat, and serve.
- **To help determine a serving size**, use an adult hand as a guide. Here are some tips:
  ½ to 1 of your hand = 1 serving of chicken, fish, or beef (50 g to 100 g)
  2 thumbs = 1 serving of hard cheese (50 g)
  1 fist = 1 serving of salad (1 cup/250 mL)
  1 thumb tip = 1 serving of margarine (1 tsp/5mL)

מָן: לֶחֶם אַבִּירים

Manna: "grain of heaven, the bread of the mighty" (Psalm 78:24–25).

The Talmud teaches us that the phrase "bread of the mighty" (bread of "*abirim*") should rather be read as "bread of *evarim*," that is, "the bread of organs." By this, the Talmud means the bread that was directly absorbed by the 248 parts (*evarim*) of the body (*Bavli Yoma* 75b).

Manna is a type of food containing all the nurturance we need. God no longer gives us manna, but he did give us the model, the "blueprint." Now that we are no longer in the desert, we need to have the skills to make our own *lechem abirim* that will nurture all parts of our body.

What is the secret of the bread of the mighty? . . . 2, 3, 4!
2 = 2 Food Groups at Snack
3 = 3 Food Groups at Breakfast
4 = 4 Food Groups at Lunch and Dinner

Examples[2]

Breakfast

Choose foods from at least **3 Food Groups**

Example   1 grain product (e.g., slice of whole wheat toast)

1 from meat and alternatives (e.g., egg)

1 from vegetables and fruit (a banana or orange)

Lunch

Choose foods from at least **4 Food Groups**

Example   1 grain product (e.g., pita bread)

1 from meat and alternatives (e.g., tuna or salmon)

1 from vegetables (e.g., sliced red pepper) and fruit (e.g., apple)

1 milk product (e.g., cheese or a glass of milk)

Snacks

Choose foods from at least **2 Food Groups**

Example   1 grain product (e.g., one serving of baked tortilla chips)

1 from vegetables (e.g., carrot sticks) and fruit (e.g., 100 percent fruit juice)

> **"R. Hisda said: He who can eat barley bread but eats wheat bread [is guilty of waste, and therefore] violates 'Thou shalt not destroy' (Deut 20:19). R. Papa said: He who can drink beer but drinks wine [is guilty of] waste and therefore violates 'Thou shalt not destroy.' But neither of the two opinions is right. *The injunction [to care for and] not to destroy one's body has priority"* (Bavli Shabbat 140b).**

Judaism teaches us that our bodies were given to us for safekeeping, and it is our spiritual duty to protect and nurture them. The Rabbis think of food as tightly connected to the soul. Just imagine then, when you're grocery shopping, you're actually going on a spiritual mission. It certainly is not an easy mission, especially with the abundance of foods available to pick from and the growing amount of nutritional information to go through.

Shopping for Healthy Food Tips

The following are some things to consider that might make your grocery shopping a little easier:

- **Have a meal plan with a shopping list.** This will help you avoid impulse decisions and high-fat, high-salt temptations.
- **Look for the Heart and Stroke Foundation's Health Check**[TM] **symbol** on food packages. It's a quick way to let you know a product is a healthy choice.

---

[2]See chart at the end of this chapter for more detail and alternative food options.

- **Don't go shopping when you're hungry.** You'll be tempted to buy more than you need.
- **Mentally divide up your cart,** filling the largest part with vegetables, fruit, and whole grains; and the next largest section with lower-fat dairy products, lean meat, and meat alternatives.
- **Spend the maximum amount of time** in the produce, bread, meat, and dairy aisles.
- **Look for time savers** like bagged salads, ready-to-eat dips, and bagged baby carrots.
- **Read the nutrition facts table.** Choose products lower in saturated and trans fats, and lower in total fat and sodium. Aim for products higher in fiber and important nutrients, such as calcium and iron.
- **Stock up on these healthy staples**: lower-fat dairy products (skim, 1%, or 2% milk, and part-skim cheeses), whole grain cereals and breads, whole wheat pasta, brown rice, fresh or frozen vegetables and fruit, leaner meats and alternatives (such as sliced turkey, baked beans, and lean ground beef).

Remember, good nutrition does not have to be boring. On the contrary, the more we pay attention to what we eat—the more we invest time and think about it—the more it becomes enjoyable and interesting.

Traditional kashrut has taught us that there is a holy way to eat, and moreover, that how we eat is a way to bring holiness into the world. Nowadays, some Jews follow eco-kashrut (kashrut with an ecological perspective[3]), which takes kashrut beyond individual food consumption and into a consideration of our relationship with all the resources we consume. Eco-kashrut practices include avoiding pesticides that harm the earth, being aware of whether farm workers are treated fairly, and whether farm animals are allowed to lead normal lives (free-range versus penned-in conditions, least painful slaughter, etc.). Eco-kashrut teaches how to make food choices based on these principles as a way of sanctifying our total chain of consumption.

What we eat, then, really matters. It is a way for us to nurture ourselves and those around us, as well as to bring *k'dushah* into our lives and the world that we live in.

---

[3]For more information see **www.urj.org** → Torah portion → Archives by Book – Leviticus/Vayikra → Sh'mini 5763 (**http://urj.org/Articles/index.cfm?id=2909&pge_prg_id=34003&pge_id=3452**).

Alternatives and Options from Food Groups

2 = 2 Food Groups at Snack
3 = 3 Food Groups at Breakfast
4 = 4 Food Groups at Lunch and Dinner

Foods Meals	Grain Products *Look for whole grains*	Meat and Alternatives *Look for Lean Meats (10% fat or less)*	Vegetables and Fruit *Look for orange and dark green vegetables and fruit*	Milk Products *Look for lowfat milk or yogurt (2% or less)*	Other Foods *For added taste and other beverages*
Breakfast	Cereal	Egg	Fresh fruit such as oranges, bananas		
	Bread		Frozen fruit such as blueberries	Yogurt	
	Pancakes	Peanut butter	100% fruit juice no sugar added	Milk or soy beverage	
	English muffin, crumpet, bagel		Dried fruit, such as raisins	Cottage cheese	Olive oil Grape seed oil
Lunch	Pita	Tuna	Vegetables such as carrots, broccoli, red peppers, grape tomatoes	Milk or soy beverage—plain or flavored	Salad dressing as a dip
	Bread	Egg			
	Tortilla	Salmon	Fresh fruit such as kiwi, apple, grapes, melon, pomegranate		Water
	Bagel or bun	Sliced meat			
	Naan bread		Dried Fruit		
	English muffin	Chili	Salad		
	Pasta	Baked beans	Applesauce	Yogurt—container, tube, or drink	Mustard/ketchup
	Rice		Fruit cup		
	Crackers	Lentil soup	100% fruit juice no sugar added	Cheese	Salsa
	Muffins	Hummus	Vegetable cocktail	Cottage cheese	
Snacks	Crackers	Nuts	Fruit juice pops	Yogurt—container, tube, or drink	Dip—yogurt or salad dressing
	Pita	Hummus	Cut up vegetables	Milk or soy Beverage	Salsa
	Bread sticks	Dry roasted soy beans	Fresh fruit		
	Cereal		Dried fruit and fruit snacks	Cheese	Water

Conflict Resolution

A Technique for Conflict Resolution Using Validating Communication

Judaism teaches that there are a few obligations that are so important they are without measure. The reward for them too, is without measure. One of these obligations is:

הֲבָאַת שָׁלוֹם בֵּין אָדָם לַחֲבֵרוֹ

Making peace when there is strife (*Mishna Pei-ah* 1:1).

Everybody stands to gain from settling strife. Conflict resolution is a skill important for all our kids to learn since it involves hearing the pain of others, as well as our own pain. Hearing the pain of another is an act of kindness, which has great powers of healing. Children who will learn this skill will be better at understanding their own needs, naming their feelings, and understanding an important component of healthy, constructive communication: validation.

We all need to feel that we are heard and validated. When someone validates our feelings, we know immediately that they listened to us; we know that they heard our fears, our concerns, our anger, and our pain. Validating someone does not mean agreeing with them. It means communicating respect for them, and acknowledging that their opinions and feelings are legitimate.

When it comes to conflicts and disagreements, validation plays an important role. It sets the flow of communication free and allows people to open up. Validation diffuses a good amount of anger almost immediately, so that the conflicting parties can continue to speak to each other from a position of understanding and acceptance.

In the technique for validation described below, there is no victim and no culprit. Both participants are encouraged to listen to each other, validate each other's statements, and find their own solution.[4] The mediator remains totally neutral.

---

[4]Except for very small children.

Five Steps of Validation

The technique for validation has five steps:

1. Tell what happened.
2. How did you feel when that happened?
3. What would you like to stop/change?
4. What would you like the other person to do instead?
5. Can you do that?

Consider the following example in which conflict resolution is necessary and the counselor uses the validation technique:

> In a study session one morning at summer camp, a group discusses traditional Jewish attitudes toward tattoos and piercing. Deborah announces that she has a tattoo that her parents let her get. She pulls back her shirt to show a tattoo of a dove with "shalom" written above it. She says it expresses her pride in being Jewish and her hopes for peace.
>
> Steve says his grandparents were Holocaust survivors who had numbers tattooed on their arms and that Deborah is a jerk. Deborah, he says, is making a joke out of a Jewish tragedy and disrespecting herself and Judaism by getting that tattoo.
>
> Neil, who has a nose ring, counters that Steve is using Holocaust guilt to make everyone else feel bad, and that when modern kids get tattoos and piercings, they are just doing what other kids do and not mocking anything or anyone.
>
> Soon everyone is yelling at everyone else, and Steve and Neil are rolling on the floor in a fistfight.
>
> You are the counselor (or teacher in a classroom, parent at the dinner table, etc.). What do you do?

The initial step that one should take as a mediator is to ask the people who are having the conflict if they would like help, and if they are willing to try to resolve their differences together. If both are willing and ready, sit down someplace where everyone is comfortable. The mediator should sit at an equal distance from participants (not closer to one of them). Other people are encouraged to watch the conflict resolution (unless participants want privacy), but they must not interfere.

Below is a scenario in which Steve and Neil, from the above story, go through the steps of the validation technique with a mediator.

Step 1: Tell What Happened

Mediator:	Steve, please tell us what happened.
Steve:	Deborah was being mean the way she was talking about her tattoos, and when I said that hurt my feelings because my grandparents are Holocaust survivors, Neil totally took her side and said I was taking them all on a huge guilt trip, so I shoved him, and he punched me, and we got into a fight.
Mediator:	Neil, please repeat what Steve said.

Neil:	Steve said that Deborah was being mean, and that she hurt his feelings. And then I took her side and said he was taking us all on a guilt trip. Then he shoved me, I punched him, and we got into a fight.
Mediator:	Neil, please tell us what happened.
Neil:	I was really mad that Steve called Deborah a jerk, even if he didn't agree with her, and I was trying to tell Steve that getting a tattoo or a piercing wasn't something personal against him or his grandparents. I mean, I have a piercing, and even if he doesn't like it, he shouldn't use the Holocaust as an argument because that makes everyone feel guilty. He got pissed off and shoved me, so then I got even more pissed off and punched him.
Mediator	Steve, please repeat what Neil said.
Steve:	Neil said that it made him mad that I called Deborah a jerk, and that what he said wasn't anything personal against me or my grandparents, but when I use the Holocaust everyone feels guilty. That's when he said I got pissed off and shoved him, so then he got more pissed off and punched me.

Step 2: How Did You Feel When That Happened?

Mediator:	Steve, how did you feel when Neil said what he did?
Steve:	I felt like Neil was telling me I wasn't important, and that my grandparents weren't important. I mean, it was bad enough the way Deborah was going on and on about her tattoos, but when he said that, I felt like he was totally dissing me, like I don't exist or something.
Mediator:	Neil, please repeat what Steve said.
Neil:	Steve said that he felt unimportant, that his grandparents were unimportant. He felt I was dissing him, like he didn't exist.
Mediator:	Neil, how did you feel when Steve said what he did?
Neil:	I just felt like I was being blamed for something that I didn't deserve getting the blame for. I mean, when Steve started with the Holocaust, it was like he was accusing me of something really big—of disrespecting his grandparents, and lots of other people or even worse—just because I have a nose ring. I didn't disrespect them.
Mediator:	Steve, please repeat what Neil said.
Steve:	Neil said that he felt blamed for something he didn't do. That when I brought up the Holocaust, it was like I was accusing him of something huge.

Step 3: What Would You Like to Stop/Change?

Mediator:	Steve, what would you like to stop/change?
Steve:	I would like Neil to stop being so insensitive about the things that matter to me. Maybe he doesn't feel this way about things, but I do, and I wish he didn't ignore that.
Mediator:	Neil, please repeat what Steve said.

Neil:	Steve said that he wants me to stop being insensitive about the things that are important to him, even if I don't feel the same way about them.
Mediator:	Neil, what would you like to stop/change?
Neil:	I would like Steve to not play the blame-game; to not make me feel guilty about being who I am, expressing myself with jewelry or whatever the way I like.
Mediator:	Steve, please repeat what Neil said.
Steve:	Neil said that he would like me to stop blaming him; that I should let him be the way he is, the way he likes to express himself.

Step 4: What Would You Like the Other Person to Do Instead?

Mediator:	Steve, what would you like Neil to do instead?
Steve:	I would like Neil to pay more attention that some people are sensitive about these things. I don't mind his nose ring or tattoos or whatever, as long as he doesn't disrespect my feelings about the Holocaust or my grandparents.
Mediator:	Neil, please repeat what Steve said.
Neil:	Steve said that he would like me to recognize that he's sensitive about these things; that he's not against my nose ring, as long as I don't disrespect his feelings.
Mediator:	Neil, what would you like Steve to do instead?
Neil:	I'd like Steve to be more tolerant toward my opinions and the way I dress—to remember that I'm not doing this to hurt him. I do respect his feelings, as long as he respects mine and lets me be who I am and not make me feel guilty about it.
Mediator:	Steve, please repeat what Neil said.
Steve:	Neil said that I should be more tolerant about the way he is, the way he talks and dresses. That it's not against me, that I shouldn't make him feel guilty for who he is, and that he respects my feelings.

Step 5: Can You Do That?

Mediator:	Steve, can you do that?
Steve:	Yes.
Mediator:	Neil, can you do that?
Neil:	Yes.
Mediator:	Can you make a firm commitment to try to behave in the way you both have agreed?
Steve and Neil:	Yes.

As a mediator, sometimes you will not be able to reach an agreement, and things will come to a dead end. In this case, just go back one step and start over. You will only be able to progress after all the feelings have been released and validated by the two participants. Repeat the process (or parts of it) as many times as needed to get there.

Validating our own emotions, as adults who guide children, is key in order for us to be able to teach them to validate their own. In other words, we as adults need to be able to first know and name whatever feelings we are having, and then be able to reconcile those emotions in order for us to move forward in any given situation.

The following is an example in which the mediator must confront his or her own emotions before helping those in conflict with one another:

> Robbie, a 12-year-old camper, just got his third package full of candy from home. Ilan, his bunk-mate, sees this and says, "No wonder you have man-boobs and a big belly, Rob, all you do is stuff your face." Their counselor tells Ilan to lay off and leave Robbie alone.
>
> Later, when Robbie takes seconds of dessert the counselor quietly says, "Are you sure you want that Rob? You know you feel bad when the kids tease you."
>
> Rob runs out of the dining room saying, "Like it's my fault they tease me?! You're on their side too!"
> What should the counselor do now? What else could he have done?

Pretend for a minute that you are the counselor. You already know that you somehow need to validate both children: it would be great if you could ask Ilan what it is about Robbie that bothers him so much (e.g., "I'm sick and tired of Robbie complaining all the time!"); it would be wonderful if you could bring Robbie's dilemma to the fore (e.g., "I know I eat too much, but I'm homesick, and it tastes good!") And yet, you're finding it difficult to do so. For some reason, you identify with one side, in this case, the "bad" side. You secretly find yourself supporting Ilan's aggression and having negative feelings toward Robbie. What is the problem here?

You need to be able to acknowledge that this is indeed how you feel. Then, try to think, why do you think you are feeling this way? Perhaps you yourself were once an overweight child and other kids made fun of you? Perhaps that is something in your past that you consider so shameful, every reminder of it (such as Robbie's overeating) sends you flying to the roof and causes you to react not quite as you would have wished? Once you've acknowledged and validated your own emotions—once you've figured out why you feel the way you feel—only then can you move forward and start figuring out how to handle the situation in a way that is helpful to everyone, including yourself.

What Helps and What Doesn't: Ruth Versus Elkanah

An Exercise for Eliciting Group Wisdom

How many times have we heard the phrase "I really want to help, I just don't know how?" How many times have we uttered that very phrase? Truth be told, even if, during the course of our life, we were mostly successful at helping people who needed us, any one of us has probably tried to help another person at one point but wound up feeling like they didn't really do that person any good. On the flip side, most of us have had the experience of reaching out to someone for help when feeling troubled or upset but then wound up feeling even worse than before. Why is it that sometimes, despite our best intentions, we just can't seem to help? What is it that really helps someone in need of comfort? Let's examine two different biblical models in which one person tries to help another to find out the answer.

Let us consider the story of Elkanah and Chana (I Samuel 1:1–28). Chana finds herself in a painful situation. She is barren, and despite wanting desperately to give Elkanah sons, she cannot, becoming more and more disappointed with each passing year. To make matters worse, Penina, Elkanah's other wife, who is quite fertile and has bourn Elkanah several children, continuously taunts Chana for her barrenness. We are told that Elkanah loved Chana very much—he would always give her a double portion of the sacrifice to eat. Chana, however, in her great pain, could not eat. When Elkanah sees Chana's misery, he is obviously moved, and attempts desperately to comfort her, saying the following: "Chana, why do you weep? Why won't you eat? Why is your heart grieved? Am I not better to you than ten sons (I Samuel 1:8)?!" Chana, needless to say, is not comforted by Elkanah's well-meaning but, alas, somewhat insensitive words. She remains, we are told, "bitter of soul" (I Samuel 1:10).

Let us now consider the story of Naomi and Ruth (Ruth 1:1–22). Naomi, widowed of husband and bereaved of both sons in the foreign land of Moab, decides to leave and go back to her own people in the land of Judea. In bitter tears she tries to bid farewell to her two daughters-in-law (who at first wish to accompany her), doing her very best to dissuade them from coming along. "I have no more sons to give you for husbands," she tells Ruth and Orpah, "and even if I were to marry today and have children, would you really want to wait all those years for them to become adults for you to marry?!" "No," Naomi continues, wishing to bear her grief alone, not wanting to burden her two daughters-in-law, "no—do not come with me." Orpah heeds her and leaves. But Ruth will not go, and in what is surely one of the most moving statements of loyalty and faithfulness says: "Where you go, I will go, and where you lodge, I will lodge. Your people shall be my people, and your God, my God" (Ruth 1:17). We are not told directly that Naomi felt comforted. But we know, in the deepest sense possible, that Ruth indeed helped alleviate Naomi's grief.

What is the difference between Elkanah and Ruth? How can we make sure that when we try to help, we act more like Ruth and less like Elkanah? (The answer to these questions can be found after the exercise. It is best to let everyone see that they already know the answers for themselves, rather than give it away.)

We may not always feel this way, but we all know how to be like Ruth. We all have the knowledge and experience that can enable us to truly be of help to those who need us. All we have to do is tap into it. The following exercise can help achieve this.

When you introduce this exercise, tell the stories of Elkanah and Chana, and of Naomi and Ruth. Explain to participants that we all have plenty of experience with feeling overwhelmed. Hopefully, we also have experience with reaching out to get some help.

All of us, in the course of our lives, must have had experiences when we reached out for help, and like Naomi, indeed felt helped. Most likely, all of us also have those experiences when, like Chana, we reached out to someone who sincerely wished to help us, but somehow ended up making us feel worse.

This exercise will help make available to us what we have learned from these experiences.

An Exercise: Remembering Our Elkanahs and Our Ruths

Materials: You will need pens or pencils and paper, as well as two large flip charts and markers.

Remember Your Ruths

Ask participants to remember a time when they were distressed (either when they were under a tremendous amount of pressure, or a time when they felt without hope, very confused, or even that they had done something not so constructive). Now try to remember, at that time of distress, reaching out for help to someone who tried to help, and like Ruth, DID help. Give people enough time to remember the situation; what was your life like at the time? What was the problem? Who was your Ruth, that person you turned to for help?

Have each participant write down the following on their own piece of paper and answer it: *What did your Ruth say or do? How did you end up feeling about yourself and about the situation/problem you were facing?*

Remember Your Elkanahs

Now ask participants to envision the exact opposite situation, that is, feeling distressed, reaching out to someone who, like Elkanah, tried to help and yet not feeling helped, perhaps even ending up feeling worse. Have each participant write down the following on their own piece of paper and answer it. *What did your Elkanah say or do? How did you end up feeling about yourself and about the situation/problem you were facing?*

When people have finished writing, ask them to share what they've written about their Elkanahs and their Ruths; sum up by reiterating the information on two large flip charts (preferably use two different colors—one for the positive experience, one for the negative).

Explain that what we want to do here is to elicit our shared wisdom gained through life-experiences, so that we can all see that in order to help someone, we do not have to be mental health specialists. Helping someone means giving them support and reassurance, and not necessarily immediate advice; helping means offering encouragement, believing in the person, and not minimizing their experience.

Elkanah wanted desperately to help Chana, but what he really did was bombard her with unnecessary questions, insist that her grief was uncalled for and that her pain was unnecessary, and then offer her the "perfect" solution: "You should be satisfied with me," he argued, "I'm better than ten sons!" Ruth, however, did not interrupt, interrogate, or argue with Naomi. She simply listened to her. She didn't tell Naomi that her pain was stupid, nor did she offer a quick solution. She simply said, in the plainest sense possible, "I'm with you."

Stress that each and every one of us, despite wanting very badly to help someone, sometimes acted like Elkanah. That is okay. That does not make us bad people who are incapable of helping people; it makes us human beings who want to help but sometimes might not know how.

The point of this exercise is to make us more aware of how much wisdom we already possess within us, so that we can access it when someone approaches us with a problem, as well as teach others to tap into their own unique sources of knowledge and experience when they are distressed.

Exercises for Expressing Emotions and Coping with Fear

Our ability to cope with stress increases greatly when we are able to identify and express a variety of emotions. But in order to fully and appropriately give expression to emotional situations we must first increase our emotional vocabulary. The aim of the following exercises is therefore to help us learn how to identify the flow of our emotions and the ways we express them through different forms of behavior, and in varied social situations.

Think again of Hagar (see "Opening Meditation on *Resilience of the Soul*" on page iii), a mother sitting at a distance from her dying son. Hagar, we are told, does not want to see her child die, and so she sits remotely, not knowing what else to do, and she bursts into tears. In this case, even though Hagar does not have the ability to solve her predicament, she is a good example of someone who can give expression to her acute pain; she is not frozen in shock, unable to respond. Rather, Hagar cries, and with a loud voice at that. Consequently, Hagar and Ishmael's pain is heard by God, and the angel of God is able to offer her help. When we express feeling and another hears us and soothes us, we are already a step ahead of where we were a mere moment before. Someone who hears our pain and reassures us can help us remember how we coped in the past; moreover, this person can help us remember that we *have* coped in the past! We are then better able to see our sources of sustenance and, like Hagar, are one step closer to handling our difficult situation.

The research literature on resilience teaches us that an empathic environment is key to resilience building. Thus, the following exercises, focusing on expression of emotions, often difficult ones, will hopefully pave the way to further development of a more empathic environment in our synagogues.

Fear and anxiety merit special attention. Being able to talk about our fears is one way to defuse their potency. Additionally, being able to look at those fears in the open often leads the way to coping and finding solutions. We often worry that working on fears will exacerbate them. It is important to note that expressing fear either verbally or through some creative outlet does not increase fear (nor does it eliminate it), but rather opens up the path

Adapted from Naomi Baum, Bamberger, and Kerem, "Building Resilience in the Classroom," an unpublished manual developed at the Temmy and Albert Latner Israel Center for the Treatment of Psychotrauma at Herzog Hospital, Jerusalem.

to enriching our efforts in coping with our emotions. It makes little difference what the source of fear actually is; it can be fear of war, fear of crossing the street, fear of people falling out of burning buildings, or fear of not being invited to the prom. Whatever it is we may be coping with merits attention, nurturance, and thought.

Allowing our emotions—no matter how negative or scary they can be—into the synagogue setting lets our teens (and their families) feel that they are not alone. It lets them know there are caring individuals who will listen to them; who are capable of containing their emotions when those become overwhelming for them.

The psalms are a pertinent example of a speaker who expresses intense emotions and then feels a sense of relief; often the psalmist finds himself in utter despair. "O God of my praise," he implores, "do not keep aloof . . . for I am poor and needy, and my heart is pierced within me. I fade away like a lengthening shadow; I am shaken off like locusts" (Psalm 109). Sometimes the psalmist goes on with a reverberation of emotions so intense it makes even our drama-saturated ears perk up in surprise. No human feeling goes untouched, including bitter anger, wrenching disappointment, vicious vengefulness, despair, revulsion, and anxiety. Expressing intense emotion has been a part of our tradition for millennia.

When you run this program in your synagogue, you may want to mention that expressing our emotions and our pains can be a scary thing. Remember that running such a program or doing such an exercise may enable some kids to express things they were not able to express before, so make sure you make yourself available and give the person positive feedback for having told you. If you feel the situation is more than you can handle, continue listening and refer to other colleagues or to a professional for further care. Most importantly, in no case make the person feel bad for having told you.

When people are able to name their fears, they may discover there is something in their lives that they need help with. Encourage the person to ask for help. Inquire: "who have you spoken to about this?" You may suggest some people yourself, such as mental health professionals, a counselor, or someone else that you trust. The point is to avoid a feeling of helplessness and powerlessness.

Victor Frankl, relaying his experiences as a prisoner in a concentration camp in his book *Man's Search for Meaning*, spoke of the importance of being connected in a meaningful way to others and of being involved in a relationship that allows a person to express a sense of decency as key to his or her survival. You will hopefully survive your situation and, like Frankl, go far beyond mere survival. It is helpful, though, to keep in mind the words of Franklin D. Roosevelt, who taught us that the only thing we have to fear is fear itself. When we deal with fear, we can cope with so much more than we thought we could. Unexpressed fear becomes paralyzing.

Exercise 1: I Feel, I Think, I Do

The goal of this exercise is to encourage expression and discussion on emotionally related subjects.

Materials

- An open space that can be used as a stage.
- "How Do I Look or Act When . . ." scenarios. Write each one on a piece of paper.
- "I Think, I Feel, I Do " worksheets (page 124).

The following is a list of possible "How Do I Look or Act When . . ." scenarios. Feel free to choose scenes from the lives of teens both at home and school. Try to make the scenes as relevant as possible. You may ask participants to add scenarios of their own choosing.

- "I get a C on my exam."
- "A kid at school is being mean to me."
- "I eat half a cheesecake because I'm emotional over something that happened at school."
- "I'm not doing as well as the other kids preparing for my bar/bat mitzvah."
- "I'm at a school party."
- "I win at sports."
- "I see a picture of a skinny model in a magazine."
- "I think my friends don't really care about me."
- "I think about terrorism."
- "I walk down the street and see a stranger in the darkness."
- "I worry about my parents being ill."
- "I get invited to a party but my best friend doesn't."
- "I go shopping with my friend and nothing fits her."
- "I am asked to join a basketball game but my brother isn't."

Instructions

1. Photocopy the "I Think, I Feel, I Do" worksheets (page 124) and hand them out to the participants.
2. Explain to the participants that in today's exercise we will learn how certain situations influence how we feel and think, and how our thoughts and feelings influence our behavior. Ask for volunteers to act out some of the various "How Do I Look or Act When . . ." scenarios. After each skit, ask participants to fill out a section on the worksheet that they have received.
3. After each skit, discuss the variety of reactions people may have to the same situation. You can note that even difficult incidents can sometimes arouse thoughts, feelings, and behaviors that display positive coping in the face of a difficult situation.

I Think, I Feel, I Do
Student Worksheet

Complete the following sentences after each skit.

Skit presented by: _____

Subject: _____

When something happens to me like that:

I think _____

I feel _____

I do _____

Skit presented by: _____

Subject: _____

When something happens to me like that:

I think _____

I feel _____

I do _____

Skit presented by: _____

Subject: _____

When something happens to me like that:

I think _____

I feel _____

I do _____

Skit presented by: _____

Subject: _____

When something happens to me like that:

I think _____

I feel _____

I do _____

Skit presented by: _____

Subject: _____

When something happens to me like that:

I think _____

I feel _____

I do _____

Exercise 2: The Many Faces of Fear

The goal of this exercise is to learn how to be less overwhelmed by fear by getting to know fear more closely.

Option 2: If you wish, you can choose a slightly different variation to this exercise titled The *Tsar* (narrow) Place in Your Life. This can allow you to focus on a variety of different emotions, and not just on fear.

Materials

Creative materials such as different kinds of crayons, paper, musical instruments, clay, play dough, scraps of material, bits of plastic, wood and metal, cotton, glue, and scissors.

If you have enough space, you may add other items connected with expressive movement, such as ribbons, skipping ropes, and crepe paper strips.

Instructions

Option 1:

1. Explain to participants that we are going to talk about fears. Every one of us has fears. We usually don't like to talk about our fears, but prefer to keep them under wraps. However, today we are going to see what happens when we actually talk about and work with our fears. What we have found is that when we look at fear directly it often changes. Fear becomes less scary if we stay with it long enough and don't run away. Something happens. Let's see what that is.
2. Consider starting the activity with an extended breathing exercise (see "Relaxation Techniques" on page 131).
3. Tell the participants, "Everyone sit comfortably on a chair, breathe in slowly . . . slowly, hold the air in, then slowly blow it out. Good. Let's do it again, nice and slow, inhale, exhale. . . . Nice . . . and once again. . . . Now I'm going to ask everyone to imagine 'fear.' If you wish, you may close your eyes, to help you imagine better. It doesn't have to be the thing that scares you the most. Look at this fear in your imagination. What color is it? What shape? How does it move? At what pace? Listen to the fear. What sound does it make? If it had a voice what would it say? Touch the fear in your imagination. What does it feel like? How does it smell?"
4. Tell the participants, "From the materials available, create your fear in any way you choose." Give the participants five to ten minutes to do so.
5. For the follow-up discussion, ask participants to share in pairs or in small groups what they have created.
6. After sharing, invite them back for a group discussion. Ask the following questions:
   - What was it like to create "fear"?
   - What was hard and what was easy for you?
   - What did you learn about fear? What did you learn about yourself?
   - Did your feelings about fear change at all during the exercise?
   - What will you take with you from this exercise?

If you prefer, prepare a worksheet, and have participants write the answers to these questions, inviting those who wish to share their answers with the group to do so.

Option 2:

1. Ask participants to think of the narrow places in their lives, places where they felt stuck.
2. You can choose to do midrash in art or midrash in story. Give participants part of a biblical narrative relating to slavery in Egypt. Explain that the name *Mitzrayim*, which is Hebrew for Egypt, comes from the root *tsar*, narrow.
3. Explain that we all have narrow places in our lives, and that you don't always exit the narrow place directly to someplace better. Sometimes we escape them only to go into a long period in the desert, like the Israelites.
4. Ask the participants, "What was your narrow place? What would your promised land be? Would you sometimes want to go back to the narrow place because you find it easier?"

Exercise 3: The Fan

The goals of this exercise are as follows:

1. To uncover the subjectivity within the definition of *stressful situations* as well as to determine what is common to them.
2. To allow participants to express themselves without having to openly expose their identity.
3. To develop awareness of the different elements that constitute stress.

Instructions

1. Prepare a sheet of paper titled "A Stressful Situation for Me Is . . ."
2. Pass the paper around from one person to the next with each one adding his or her own ending to the statement. Each person should fold the paper after writing an answer so that the rest of the class cannot read what he or she wrote. The paper can be folded back and forth, like a fan. If you have a large class pass around several sheets of paper.
3. Once everyone has had a chance to respond, have one person volunteer to unfold the fan and read each sentence. At the same time write all the sentences on the board or on a sheet of paperboard.
4. Hold a discussion after you have formed a general picture of the whole group. The following are possible points for discussion:
   - How did you find the writing process?
   - Is it possible to create categories from the responses? If not, why? (Possible answers: the categories are *personal, unique,* and *one off.*) If yes, what categories can be created? (Possible answers: *sentences that emphasize physical characteristics, behavioral, emotional, metaphoric,* and *concrete.*)
   - What does having a variety of names for emotions mean to you? (Possible answer: *having a sense of order in the confusion that is known as "stressful situations" may help ease the coping.*)
5. If you have enough time, you can pass around two pieces of paper. The second one can have the heading, "When I'm Stressed, I Turn To . . ."

Exercise 4: Line-Color-Shape

The goal of the exercise is to become acquainted with a range of emotions and to find creative expression for them.

Materials

- Drawing paper
- Colored pencils or crayons

Instructions

1. Ask participants to help list a series of feelings and their opposites. Use weak and strong as the first example. Write the pairs on the blackboard. The following are suggested feeling pairs:
   - Weak and Strong
   - Sociable and Aggressive
   - Tough and Soft
   - Sad and Happy
   - Angry and Calm
   - Tense and Relaxed

2. Ask each participant to think of how he or she can express emotions through colors and shapes. Think of which color or shape fits each emotion.
3. Ask each participant to pick one or two pairs of concepts and to draw a picture of them using the color and shape they find most suited to the emotion.
4. When they have finished drawing, have them show their drawings to the others, either in small groups or in one larger group. You may hang up an exhibition grouping the pictures by emotions.
5. Follow this with a discussion based on the following questions:
   - Are there similar shapes and colors for the same emotions?
   - Are there different shapes and colors for the same emotions?
   - What factors determine the choice of line, color, and shape of a particular emotion?
6. (Optional) Ask everyone to add captions to their drawings and make a class collage from them.

Creating Your Own Blessing: Joint Activity for Teens and Parents

Reciting a blessing allows us to open ourselves to God's presence in our lives. Perhaps we are not used to God's presence; perhaps we don't know what God's presence even means. Even if we feel disconnected from God, even if we feel God is irrelevant to our lives, the act of blessing is one of turning to that which is beyond our ability to understand. When asking for a blessing, we recognize our limitations, and through that, open ourselves to possibilities we did not even think of before.

We all have hopes and dreams. We all have fears and needs. Blessing and prayer are the starting point of a dialogue about those hopes, dreams, fears, and needs. It is a private dialogue between us and God. It helps to give ourselves permission to be personal in our prayers.

We start by remembering the traditional blessing formula (*Baruch atah Adonai, Eloheinu Melech haolam, asher . . . ,* "Blessed are You, *Adonai*, Sovereign of the universe, who has . . .") and think about what names we choose for God, *Adonai*. We define for ourselves what God's power, qualities, and attributes are. We state the act, event, or circumstance for which we want a blessing, and finally, we reiterate God's ability to act in the world.

Consider using this model to create the blessing you need now:

1. (Naming God) Blessed are You, _____

2. (Quality and attribute) who _____

3. (Event) be with me as _____

4. (God's ability to act) Blessed are you who _____

_____

Adapted from Marcia Cohn Spiegel, "Creating Your Own Blessing," in *Traditions—The Complete Book of Prayers, Rituals, and Blessings for Every Jewish Home*, by Sara Shendelman and Avram Davis (Boston: Hyperion, 1998).

Relaxation Techniques

Relaxation is an excellent way of decreasing tension, bringing about a feeling of calmness and control, and enhancing a balance of peace and mind. Among other things, relaxation techniques allow the body to rejuvenate and replenish itself by releasing muscle tension and clearing the mind of worries and other troubling thoughts.

Much research has documented the beneficial effects of regularly practicing relaxation, including lowering blood pressure, increasing concentration, increasing energy, and creating a general feeling of well-being. Below are a number of different exercises. They are simple to practice and help reduce tension and stress. There is no one "correct" way to relax. Try several of these exercises at least once before deciding which ones you prefer. You can use them during a special *t'filah* service, during a parent-teen meeting, in religious school, at summer camp, or hand them out for people to try at home. Try no more than one or two different exercises per day.

Children, in general, relax easily and have fewer resistances than do adults to learning active relaxation techniques. Adapting various relaxation exercises to the classroom environment can be one of the easiest and most productive exercises a teacher or youth leader can choose.

If your congregation is not accustomed to practicing relaxation techniques in the synagogue, you can expect some puzzled looks. However, you will find that after the initial discomfort has passed (or excited giggling in the case of younger people), exercising relaxation will feel more and more natural. In the case of a group of teens, as in most groups, there will be a few who actively resist the exercises. The best way to approach this resistance is to expect it, and include it in your directions. For example, rather than saying "everybody close your eyes," you might say, "some of you may like to close your eyes, others may like to keep your eyes open." You might add, "If you prefer, you can simply place your head on your desk and use these few minutes to rest. The only rule is no noise and no disturbing your neighbors." The more experiences they will have with relaxation, the more you will find participants relaxing readily and enjoying the break in routine.

It is highly recommended that you try out these exercises on yourself several times before bringing them to your synagogue, youth group, camp, etc. The more comfortable you are with them, the more comfortable the group will be with them.

Adapted from Naomi Baum, Bamberger, and Kerem, "Building Resilience in the Classroom," an unpublished manual developed at the Temmy and Albert Latner Israel Center for the Treatment of Psychotrauma at Herzog Hospital, Jerusalem.

The following sections describe three relaxation techniques for a group setting and three relaxation exercises to practice by oneself.

Relaxation Techniques for a Group Setting

Relaxation Meditation: *N'shamah/N'shimah*[5]

Breathing is a primary component of any relaxation technique. The following guided meditation is designed to help people relax. It can be used either with adults or teens, or both. The participants should be in seated or prone positions in a darkened room. They should be comfortable and should close their eyes if they feel comfortable doing so.

The leader, someone who has familiarized him- or herself with this exercise, should read the following script in a calm voice:

"Begin breathing. Inhale through the nose. Keep the mouth closed and exhale through the nose. Slow your breath down to a 5 count. Inhale 1-2-3-4-5. Exhale 1-2-3-4-5." Repeat the breathing and counting several times.

"The only sounds you should hear should be your breath and the sound of my voice. Let all other sounds and thoughts pass through your mind. Acknowledge them and then let them float away as if on a cloud. Always return to the sound of your breath. Breathe in, breathe out.

"As you focus on your breath, think about the words *n'shimah* and *n'shamah*. *N'shimah* is the Hebrew word for *breath* and *n'shamah* is the Hebrew word for *soul*. How did *Adonai* create? By breathing breath into the first human being made from dust from the four corners of the earth. Remembering God's breath, breathe in, breathe out.

"Each breath we take allows us to create and re-create our soul, our *n'shamah*. It allows us to re-create each cell in our body, as the energy, the Godliness, enters our body and leaves our body; enters our body and leaves our body. We breathe a bit of God into our souls and when we exhale, we release that God energy into the world. Breathe in, breathe out.

"On each inhalation take from the energy in the room whatever you need—calmness, strength, courage—whatever you need from the universe. On each exhalation, breathe out all the goodness you have to offer the world. Breathe in, breathe out.

"Continue breathing and re-creating your cells and your *n'shamah* for a few minutes. If your mind wanders, just return to your breath."

After a few minutes, say the following:

"Breathe in, breathe out. Begin to feel sensation returning to your body. Wiggle your fingers and toes, bend your knees. Roll over on your right side. Take a few more breaths with your eyes closed. Push yourself up into a seated position. Breathe. Feel

---

[5]This relaxation meditation was provided by Rabbi Susie Heneson Moskowitz. Rabbi Moskowitz has integrated meditation and yoga in creating and leading innovative worship services, including one she led at the URJ Biennial in Houston in 2005.

God's *n'shimah* coursing through your *n'shamah*. Feel a sense of calmness and renewal and an ability to face the challenges of life. Look down at your lap and slowly open your eyes. Look up and out at the beauty within each person in the room. Shalom."

Minute Meditation

This relaxation exercise takes about sixty seconds. It is a wonderful way to begin a class, workshop session, or use as a break between strenuous activities.

Have the participants sit in their seats and close their eyes. Once they are seated, read the following instructions slowly in a calm voice. Wait about fifteen to twenty seconds between each stage.

"Notice how you are sitting on your chair. How your back touches the back of the chair. Feel your shoes on the floor and your feet inside them. Place your hands on your legs.

"Listen to your breathing. Notice the air you inhale and exhale. Inhale again, more slowly, and let the air out. Notice the way your body is feeling.

"Do a body scan. Review your body from head to toe. Ask yourself: 'What is my stress level? Relaxation level? How worried am I? What are my expectations? Hopes?'" (Feel free to adapt the questions to your needs.)

"When you are ready, return to the room, to the group, and open your eyes slowly."

A Journey through the Body: Full Body Relaxation

This exercise is suitable for all ages. If you wish, you can add music in the background that is soothing and relaxing. Most people enjoy having music in the background, although there are some that find it distracting.

Please note that these are suggested texts for getting started. Feel free to depart from them and use your own words.

The leader should begin the exercise by saying:

"Now we're going to do a relaxation exercise that will help us all calm down and feel better. I'd like everyone to sit quietly and get comfortable in their chair. Listen to my instructions."

Read the instructions in a slow, quiet voice, pausing often between sentences.

"Close you eyes and listen to the rhythm of your breathing. Now, let's release all the muscles in our bodies and let them relax. Relax your feet, your legs, the palms of your hands, your shoulders and neck, and your face. Breathe very slowly. If you'd like, you can tense all your muscles, and then let them go. Tense all your muscles. Make fists with your hands. Scrunch up your face. Tighten your shoulders and legs. Hold it, hold it. Now let go, and take a slow, deep breath.

"We're about to set off on a journey through our bodies. Let's move very slowly. Try to feel each and every muscle and bone in your body.

"Start with your hands. Visualize your right hand from the tip of your pinky through all your fingers, all the way up to your elbow and from there to your right shoulder.

Everywhere you go continue to breathe deeply, and visualize your body parts letting go, relaxing, becoming softer, warmer, heavier. Move around to your left shoulder and down to your left arm. From there move to you wrist and hand and fingers. Move back up to your shoulders, and slowly go up your neck. Continue relaxing into each part of your body. Move up to your head. Move around your head to your scalp and to your forehead, your eyebrows, eyes, ears, lips, and mouth. Now move to your chin and back again to your neck and shoulders. Go back through the cavity of your chest. Notice your heartbeat. Move to your solar plexus and to your stomach. Notice what you feel there. Notice how your whole body is relaxing, feeling warm, feeling good.

"Now move down your right leg to the knee, the ankle, the heel, the ball of your foot, and your toes. Now move to your left leg. Down to the knee, ankle, heel, ball of your foot, and to the end of your toes.

"Now your whole body is feeling relaxed and calm. Stay with that feeling for a moment or two, and enjoy it. Remember that you can come back here whenever you wish. Now, move out slowly and quietly. Begin to let your eyes flutter. Move your fingers and toes. Slowly, very slowly, come back here, to the classroom, to your chair."

Allow a few moments for everyone to get their bearings before continuing. The first few times you try this exercise, you may ask participants to volunteer their experiences. Remember that there is no right or wrong way to respond. If certain people express difficulties in following the exercise, assure them that it is a matter of practice and that with time they will become more proficient in relaxation.

Relaxation Exercises to Practice by Oneself

How to begin practicing relaxation techniques by yourself:
It is important to find a comfortable, relaxed position while you engage in each of these exercises. For many people, a good way to begin is by sitting in a chair upright, with feet on the floor and hands resting on the thighs. However, if you find that this position is uncomfortable for you, sit or lie down in another pose. You may continue the exercises for as long as you want; some people simply continue until they are ready to finish and others like to preset an alarm clock. Try to spend at least five minutes on any one exercise. You may build up to thirty minutes or more, if you so desire. In order to complete each exercise, slowly begin to move your hands and feet, take five deep breaths, and open your eyes. It's very important to end each exercise gently and calmly, so that you can carry with you the effect of the relaxation for the rest of the day.

It is very important to remember, though, that relaxation techniques do not work for everybody. Note how you feel when you try them. If they make you feel more agitated, restless, or worried than you felt before, don't do them!

Exercise A

Take a deep breath. Inhale through your nose and exhale through your mouth. While you are slowly exhaling, close your eyes and feel yourself beginning to relax. Think about the phrase Jews recite every morning as part of the daily prayer, "God, the soul You have given me is pure." Take a short break between breaths and continue to breathe in through your nose and out through your mouth, thinking of your breath being pure. Notice the rhythm of your inhalations and exhalations. You can try to gently imagine the word *pure* each time you exhale. Keep your eyes closed and continue the exercise for a few minutes.

Exercise B

This progressive muscle relaxation contrasts tension and relaxation in the body. Close your eyes. Focus your attention on your head. Scrunch up your eyes, forehead, nose, and mouth. Maintain this pose for a few seconds and then relax your face. Repeat this action again, except this time, relax only half your face, but hold the other half still in its former position. Hold this position for a few seconds and then relax completely.

Now focus your attention on your shoulders, and repeat the exercise while moving down your body. Make a fist out of your left hand and bend your elbow inwards as far as you can, so that your fist touches your left shoulder. Feel the tension in your arm while you hold this position for a few seconds. Relax and let your hand return to its position on your thigh. Pay attention to the sensation in your muscles as they tense and release. Repeat with your right arm.

After clenching your shoulders, repeat the tension and relaxation exercise in your stomach, hips, thighs, shins, and feet. Breathe deeply and hold each position for a few seconds. Relax all the tension at once as you exhale. Notice the tension leaving your body.

Exercise C

Warmth and relaxation go hand in hand. Another way to feel relaxed is to feel warmer. Think of the term "Sh'chinah," the feminine presence of God in Jewish tradition. Think about the wings of *Sh'chinah* and what it would be like to lie under the wings of the *Sh'chinah*. Lie on a couch or bed and imagine that you are lying beneath the soft wings of *Sh'chinah*. Imagine those wings like a warm, heavy blanket covering your feet. Feel the warmth they provide. Imagine that the wings are slowly rolling upwards, shielding and covering your legs, then your stomach, then your chest. Feel the warmth climbing up and spreading through your limbs, helping you feel more and more relaxed.

Additional Resources

- Benson, Herbert, Ann Benson, and Ann MacDonald. *Mind Your Heart: A Mind/Body Approach to Stress Management, Exercise, and Nutrition for Heart Health.* New York: Free Press, 2004.
- Benson, Herbert, and Miriam Klipper. *The Relaxation Response.* New York: HarperCollins, 2000.
- Benson, Herbert, Eileen M. Stuart, et al. *Wellness Book: The Comprehensive Guide to Maintaining Health and Treating Stress-Related Illness.* New York: Simon and Schuster, 1993.
- Kaplan, Aryeh. *Jewish Meditation: A Practical Guide.* New York: Schocken, 1995.
- Lew, Alan. *Be Still and Get Going: A Jewish Meditation Practice for Real Life.* New York: Little, Brown and Company, 2005.

Exercises for Making Meaning and Finding Hope for the Future

When we go through difficult times, one of the questions that tends to recur in our minds is "Why are these difficult things happening to me?" Human beings are meaning-seeking creatures, and so it is only natural that we try not only to make sense of our difficulties, but also to attach some kind of higher significance to them. In a synagogue setting, allowing a shared discussion of this difficult question "Why is this happening to me?" even when we don't have the answer, can create a sense of community and build a network of mutual support, which is perhaps the most important component of resilience. We can find comfort and encouragement by finding meaning in our actions and in our experiences, each and every one in his or her own unique way, within his or her unique family and community.

Focusing on hope is vital in dealing with difficult situations. When we have hope, we are more resilient. In Jewish tradition, the communal sense of hope (traditionally, hope for the messianic age), much like in the known expression "the light at the end of a tunnel," is also expressed through an image of light. As part of the daily prayer service, we recite "*or chadash al tzion tair*";

אוֹר חָדָשׁ עַל צִיּוֹן תָּאִיר וְנִזְכֶּה כֻלָּנוּ מְהֵרָה לְאוֹרוֹ

Let a new light shine upon Zion; soon, may every one of us be reflected in its light.

Even though it applies to the messianic age, the "new light" can also be taken to express that tiny spark, that invaluable glimmer of hope that each of us needs to nurture in our hearts at all times so that it can sustain us and illuminate our days in our darker periods, helping us to pull through to better times.

Adapted from Naomi Baum, Bamberger, and Kerem, "Building Resilience in the Classroom," an unpublished manual developed at the Temmy and Albert Latner Israel Center for the Treatment of Psychotrauma at Herzog Hospital, Jerusalem.

The following two exercises focus on aspects of building resilience:

Exercise 1: The Manna in the Desert

The goal of this exercise is to try to find the positive in a negative situation.

Materials

Student worksheet (page 139).

Instructions

1. Explain that we are going to do an exercise to help us practice finding the good even in difficult situations. In every difficult situation, time period, or event there can be found some moments that give us strength and hope; moments that make us feel that we are learning something important about ourselves, about the people around us, or about the world in general. The Israelites walked the desert for forty years. During that time, they suffered hunger, thirst, loneliness, and loss of faith. And yet even that difficult situation had some good in it: the Israelites had daily proof that they were being taken care of, and it came in the form of manna from heaven. Tell the group that we all have moments we can think of as moments of manna in the desert.

2. Ask each participant to think of an unpleasant incident or situation he or she went through, in which they found some meaningful moments or in which they were taught something important and encouraged to go on.

3. Give each participant a worksheet (page 139). Ask them to write down what happened to them and answer the questions about the special insights they gained. Encourage all participants to write out their experience. There will be those who ask if they have to write. They should be encouraged to do so. There is evidence in the research literature that points to the therapeutic effect of writing, and participants will be able to process their personal stories more deeply when asked to write about them.

4. After five to ten minutes, ask for volunteers to share their story and their manna, something important that encouraged them to go on. This sharing process is usually very moving and meaningful for the group as a whole. It is very important to have no side conversations during this time, so that each person has the time and respect to share his or her story.

The Manna in the Desert
Student Worksheet

Describe an unpleasant event or situation you experienced.

_____

_____

_____

_____

What did you lean from that moment? What was the manna in the desert for you?

_____

_____

_____

_____

What have you learned from that particular moment in time that you have taken with you?

_____

_____

_____

_____

If you met someone else who was about your age today, from another country, who is going through a difficult time, what would you tell him or her about how you have learned to cope with a difficult situation?

_____

_____

_____

_____

Exercise 2: When Peace Arrives

The goal of this exercise is to focus on a sense of hope and build optimism for peace in the future.

Try to focus on a notion of peace as more than just "the absence of war." What would it mean to have inner peace? What would it look like?

There are two options for this exercise. Both are listed below.

Option 1: Isaiah's Vision

Materials

- Writing paper
- Pencils and pens
- Crayons, markers, and assorted arts and crafts materials

Instructions

1. Explain that we will be talking about our hopes and prayers for the future.
2. Read out the following verses from the vision of the Prophet Isaiah.

   Isaiah 2:2–4
   And it shall be, in the last days the mountain of the Lord's house shall be established in the top of the mountains, and shall be exalted above the hills; and all nations shall flow into it. And many people shall go and say, Come, and let us go to the mountain of the Lord, to the house of the God of Jacob. And He will teach us of His ways, and we will walk in His paths. For out of Zion shall go out the Law and the Word of the Lord from Jerusalem. And He shall judge among the nations, and shall rebuke many people; and they shall beat their swords into plowshares, and their spears into pruning-hooks. Nation shall not lift up sword against nation; neither shall they learn war any more.

   Isaiah 11:6
   The wolf also shall dwell with the lamb, the leopard shall lie down with the young goat, the calf and the young lion and the fatling together; and a little child shall lead them.

3. Explain to the participants that these quotes from Isaiah describe the prophet's vision and prayers for a future of peace. Ask everyone to draw (or make with other supplies) their hope and prayers for the future, their own version of peace.
4. After the group has had ten or so minutes to work on their visions, ask everyone to share their hopes and prayers.
5. If there is time, and you would like to have a group project as well, divide participants into smaller groups and have them make crafts from the materials, conveying the group's wishes for the future.
6. If you have the opportunity to do so, display the objects in an exhibit.

Option 2: Noah's Ark

Materials

- The Story of Noah's Ark

- Large roll of paper/poster sized paperboard
- Magic markers and crayons

Instructions

1. Tell the story of Noah's Ark and the dove of peace (Genesis 6:9–8:14) either from the original, or by heart.
2. When you have finished telling the story, lay down a large roll of paperboard (if you are working with a large group, consider dividing it into smaller groups—each gets their own paperboard), and all the crayons. Ask all the participants to write and draw their associations on the subject of hope that arise from the story.
3. At the end of the exercise a huge poster will have been created that will express how everyone relates to the subject of hope. A discussion or presentation can be held about the project.
4. We recommend hanging or putting up the project. If there was more than one group, each group can provide a name for the other group's poster.

Keeping a Creative Journal

An Approach for Managing Stress

Our tradition is one of storytelling. Our ancestors deemed passing on the stories that were passed on to them, the stories of our people, to be of utmost importance. We know this because their combined efforts resulted in what we today know as Torah. Just think of the ritual of Torah reading. We take out the draped scroll, embrace it in our arms, and reverently parade it around the sanctuary—singing and clapping for all to see and touch and share in. The symbolism of passing the Torah is indeed a powerful one. It reminds us that we all share in the stories of our tradition, future, past, and present. It also reminds us that telling stories, our stories, really matters.

Aside from laying down the building blocks for future traditions, written words have also been used by peoples throughout history to liberate themselves from thoughts and feelings that were burdening them. Writing has aided individuals in releasing that which was troublesome from heart and mind. King David wrote psalms of pain and anguish when his soul was fraught with overwhelming emotions. Anne Frank sustained herself through confiding in her trusted journal about life in a tiny hiding place with no privacy and under constant threat. Both of these individuals knew what we know today: journaling can have a curative effect, helping to free the soul and the body, and even strengthen the immune system.

Brian Luke Seaward teaches about the benefits of journaling:

> To open up, share, and disclose feelings, perceptions, opinions, and memories has always been found to be therapeutic. Confessions of the mind can lighten the burden of the soul. Many religions have adapted this concept of spiritual healing. This is also the cornerstone upon which modern psychotherapy is based. . . . Journal writing can be defined as a series of written passages that document the personal events, thoughts, feelings, memories, and perceptions in the journey throughout one's life leading to wholeness.[6]

Journaling is helpful for more than simply documenting one's life; in fact, you can think of journaling as a much-needed cleansing product, helping clear the mind's sensors that are

---

[6]Brian Luke Seaward, *Managing Stress: A Creative Journal*, 3rd ed. (Boston: Jones and Bartlett Publishers, 2004), p. xiii.

in stimulation overload from living a hectic twenty-first century life. More relevantly, you can think of journaling as a kind of rebooting of your system—much like in the case of a frozen computer—it forces you to stop and clear out all the unnecessary clutter so that you can start "operating" more smoothly.

Journaling is great to use as a complementary resource to relaxation techniques (see "Relaxation Techniques" on page 131), because relaxation can help with the symptoms of stress, and journaling, a more reflective tool, can help acquaint us with the sources of the stressors in our lives. When keeping a journal over a prolonged period of time, we can begin to notice repetitive patterns in our lives. We can see patterns in the way that we think, in our emotional responses, in our spiritual ebb and flow, and in the ways we behave. Journaling regularly can open a door into the unexpected since, as Seaward explains, "when pen or pencil is taken in hand and put to paper, a connection is made between the mind and the soul."[7] Learning from the symbolism of passing the Torah in the sanctuary, we would do well to remind ourselves that telling stories, to others as well as to ourselves, can help us heal, regroup, regain our mental acuity, and most importantly, allow us the opportunity to better know ourselves.

Journaling is a tool that can be easily integrated into almost any synagogue activity, including youth group programming, religious school sessions, and even board meetings. You can also plan a separate session based solely around journaling, during which you can teach teens and their families about its benefit, try it out, and discuss the experience.

Below are some suggested journal entry topics that can help teens and their families (but not exclusively them) reflect on relevant issues in their lives. Reflections based on the topics below can assist in alleviating stress as well as help families to gain new perspectives on familiar issues.

List your stressors. In many ways this journal entry seems to tell you something you already know all too well, that you are under stress. But when was the last time you actually sat down to truly conduct an in-depth examination of what your stress is all about? When was the last time you actually "picked stress apart," really taking the time to analyze it rather than just get through it or ignore it?

Take the time now to literally list your stressors. Write down everything that is bothering you; everything that you find troubling lately; everything that causes you to get angry, anxious, or worried. Prioritize your stressors from most to least stressful. After you have finished listing your stressors, describe in a line or two exactly how they make you feel. When you are done, allow yourself to sit down for a few minutes and simply "be" with your stressors.

Count your blessings. Here's a well-known expression we rarely, if ever, take literally. But this is exactly what you are going to do today. You are literally going to count your blessings for the day that went by. Think about your day today. It may have been wonderful. It may have been just run-of-the-mill. Or, it may have been just "one of those days" we all have every now and then when nothing goes right. Even the most difficult of days, however, has a silver lining. It isn't always easy to find, and it isn't usually a grand shining moment, but it is there nonetheless. Take this opportunity to

---

[7]Ibid., p. xiv.

count your blessings. Write a short description of each, describe how each makes you feel, and number them. (Conversely, if you find yourself in an especially dark place in your life and you feel that you are unable to connect to this journal entry, try counting your curses for the day.)

Confronting our *"Satan."* For most of us, the most common reaction to a frustrating situation is running as far away from it as possible. It is helpful, in that sense, to think of that situation, of that "it," of that adversary (in the Hebrew, literally *"Satan"*), from which you run away. In the *Hashkiveinu* prayer of the evening prayer service, we ask God *v'haser satan milfaneinu u'meahoreinu*, to "remove the adversary from before us and from behind us," thus owning up to our difficulty in facing up to the challenge alone, without assistance. But this is exactly what you are going to try to do in this journal entry; you are not going to avoid confronting your adversary anymore—be it a person, an event, or a situation—because the truth is, the harder you try to ignore it, the more it will come back to haunt you, and the more the emotional pain you are going to suffer because of it.

In his book, Seaward states that "the art of peaceful confrontation involves a strategy of creativity, diplomacy and grace to ensure that you come out the victor and not the victim."[8] Look at your stressor list from the journal entry activity described above. Pick a stressor, and map out an action plan. Write down your plan and how you're going to carry it out. Employ every ounce of creativity, diplomacy, and grace that is in you. When you are done, pretend you have already employed the solution successfully: What was your strategy? How did it work? How did it make you feel? What did you learn?

***Modim Anachnu*, We Thank You**. A particularly dramatic moment in the daily *Amidah* prayer occurs in the third to last blessing, the blessing of Thanksgiving. When we reach this blessing, it is customary to take a deep bow at the waist, almost folding at a ninety degree angle, and then to recite the blessing: "We thank You, who are *Adonai* our God and the God of our fathers and mothers. . . ." At this moment of giving thanks to God, many people take the opportunity to list all the things for which they are grateful, the things that they may not necessarily think to be grateful of, the things they may take for granted.

It is not easy giving thanks in troubled times, especially when stress clouds the mind and you cannot see straight for all the thick fog. The more we sink into our stress, the more we can feel burdened by despair, anguish, and hopelessness. Taking the time to give thanks, especially when it is furthest from our minds, can serve as a momentary breaking away from the fog of stress, a breaking away that can lead us to a way out we may not have been able to see. Take this journal entry as an opportunity to write your own *modim* blessing. What are you grateful for? What would you like to give thanks for that you usually take for granted? List as many things as you possibly can. Imagine yourself taking a deep bow whenever you add one more thing to your list.

It Is Not Good for Man to Be Alone. We are who we are because of the relationships we have in our lives. Each of us is someone's child, someone's friend, some-

---

[8] Ibid., p. 54.

one's cousin, niece, enemy, parent, and so on and so on. Relationships are central to the human experience, but relationships can also be very complicated to maintain. At some point or another, each of us has felt like someone we cherish has driven us crazy.

For this journal entry, think of someone you are in a relationship with. It can be a friend, a parent, a child, or anyone else. Think of a period or incident when that relationship made you very frustrated. For instance, it can be a time when you fought with your mom, a time when you were dumped by your girlfriend, a specific quarrel you had with someone, or a disappointment you suffered at the hand of someone you trust. Write down the general details of that event, and then write down your thoughts about it as they come to you. What feelings did you have at the time of the incident? What feelings do you have about it now? If you were to attach a soundtrack to that moment, as if it were a scene in a movie, what music would you choose?

Suggestions for When You Want to Hurt Yourself

The following are suggestions from people who self-injure about alternative activities that may prevent an episode of self-inflicted violence.[9] These suggestions may not work for everyone and are no substitute for seeking care and comfort from professionals, family members, and friends. We provide these as examples of the kinds of alternative activities those who self-injure have found effective on occasion to cope with overwhelming emotional pressures and feelings of lack of self-worth.

- Deep breathing and other relaxation techniques.
- Calling a friend, therapist, or a crisis line.
- Visiting a friend or going to a public place you enjoy.
- Taking a hot bath or shower.
- Listening to music.
- Going for a walk.
- Writing in a journal about your feelings.
- Punching a bed or a pillow (when nothing but a physical outlet for your anger and frustration will work).
- Wearing an elastic band around your wrist and snapping it when you feel you cannot control the urge to hurt yourself.
- Holding ice cubes in your hands. The cold causes pain in your hands, but it is not dangerous or harmful.
- Writing down a word best associated with what you are feeling (e.g., horrible, useless, sad, lonely, angry) and continuing to write it down, over and over. The words might look silly on the page, which may put a smile on your face.
- Drawing, painting, sculpting, singing, playing a musical instrument, or any other creative activity that can channel your emotions.
- Sharing your feelings with someone instead of keeping them private.
- Avoiding temptation by staying away from places where the things you use to hurt yourself are stored or sold.
- Taking up a sport or exercising on a consistent basis.

---

[9]Found on **http://www.mirror-mirror.org/selfinj.htm**.

- Attending religious services that are meaningful to you.
- Writing a letter (to keep for yourself or to share with a therapist or counselor) addressed to the people who have caused you pain in which you express in your own words how they made you feel.
- Doing household chores that take your mind off your feelings.
- Finding a meaningful poem, prayer, or story and reading it each time you feel overwhelmed or negative about yourself.
- Listing reasons why you are going to stop hurting yourself and reading the list every time you get the urge to start.

Section 6

Meditations, Inspirational Readings, and Prayers

Creating a Shelter of Peace

A Joint Meditation for Parents and Teens

This can be used at the beginning of a prayer service, as an opening to a joint parent-teen session, as a separate meditation exercise, etc.

Materials

Each participating family will need a tallit large enough for at least two people to wrap around themselves.

Instructions

1. Gather in a space that would allow a group of people to stand around comfortably.
2. Hum or play a *niggun* without words, so that everyone may join. You might want to teach a simple tune for the following words from the *Hashkiveinu* prayer, the final part of the evening *Sh'ma*:

וּפְרוֹשׂ עָלֵינוּ סֻכַּת שְׁלוֹמֶךָ

Ufros aleinu sukat sh'lomecha.
Spread over us the shelter of your peace.

3. Guide each family to wrap the tallit around themselves and over their heads like a tent. They will have to hug each other to do this comfortably.
4. Have each family recite the blessing said when donning a tallit:

בָּרוּךְ אַתָּה יהוה אֱלֹהֵינוּ מֶלֶךְ הָעוֹלָם אֲשֶׁר קִדְּשָׁנוּ בְּמִצְוֹתָיו וְצִוָּנוּ לְהִתְעַטֵּף בַּצִּיצִית

Baruch Atah Adonai Eloheinu Melech haolam, asher kid'shanu b'mitzvotav v'tzivanu l'hitateif batzitzit.
Blessed are You, *Adonai*, Sovereign of the universe, who has made us holy with his mitzvot, and commanded us to wrap ourselves amid the fringed tallit.

5. Continue humming together, covered.

151

6. The following is a suggested contemplation that should be read aloud to the participants:

When did everything get so complicated? Remember how easy it used to be to fix things, a skinned knee with a Band-Aid, fear of the dark with a late night story, a bruised elbow with a kiss. For the younger among us, remember how good it felt to know that someone could make things better? For the parents among us, remember how good it felt to be able to make things better?

It's not so easy anymore. Everywhere we turn something in our lives seems to need fixing. Whenever we solve one problem, another one seems to pop up in its stead. Nothing has an easy answer. There never seems to be enough time. Everything is complicated. A Band-Aid doesn't work anymore and, as we grow older, problems cannot simply be kissed away. But the power of tackling problems together, the power of the lips that touch a forehead, the power of the hand that peels the Band-Aid and gently fastens it across a bleeding gash, that power is everlasting.

We pray to God to spread over us a shelter of peace, remembering the shelter of the ongoing love between parents and children, and knowing that when we are troubled, afraid, or in pain, that shelter of ongoing love is still about us. The shelter exists even when we cannot see or feel it. Whatever else happens in our lives, when we have that shelter, we are blessed. In Jewish tradition, it is customary for parents to bless their children on Shabbat evening by placing both hands on the child's head and reciting the following:

For Boys:

יְשִׂמְךָ אֱלֹהִים כְּאֶפְרַיִם וְכִמְנַשֶּׁה

Y'simchah Elohim k'efrayim v'ki'menasheh.
May God make you like Ephraim and like Menasheh.

When Jacob blesses Ephraim and Menasheh, it is the first time a set of siblings receives a blessing together at the same time in the Torah. When we wish for our children to be like Ephraim and Menasheh, we are in essence wishing peace upon them, remembering too that we have enough blessing to suffice for all our children.

For Girls:

יְשִׂמֵךְ אֱלֹהִים כְּשָׂרָה רִבְקָה רָחֵל וְלֵאָה

Y'simaech Elohim k'sarah rivkah rachel v'leah.
May God make you like Sarah, Rebecca, Rachel, and Leah.

None of the Matriarchs had an easy life. Each endured many hardships. When we wish for our children to be like Sarah, Rebecca, Rachel, and Leah, it is not the hardships we wish on them, but rather the resilience to withstand them with inner strength and hope for the future. With their efforts, the Matriarchs built a nation; may our children build their own future with equal passion, and may we always know how to stand beside them, to support and nurture them in their chosen paths.

Perhaps you know in whose image you wish your children to be blessed. Perhaps you do not. Most essentially, we should remember to bless our children in the image of their own selves. May they always be themselves, loved and cherished for who they are.

יְבָרֶכְךָ יְהֹוָה וְיִשְׁמְרֶךָ

Yevarechecha Adonai v'yish-m'recha.
May God bless you and keep you.

יָאֵר יְהֹוָה פָּנָיו אֵלֶיךָ וִיחֻנֶּךָּ

Ya'er Adonai panav ay-lecha vi-chu-necha.
May God shine his countenance upon you and be gracious unto you.

יִשָּׂא יְהֹוָה פָּנָיו אֵלֶיךָ, וְיָשֵׂם לְךָ שָׁלוֹם

Yisa Adonai panav ay-lecha v'ya-sem l'cha shalom.
May God raise his countenance to you and grant you peace.

When we put on the tallit, we humans bless God. When we bless our children, we ask God to bless us humans. Blessing flows both ways: From the small to the large and from the large to the small. Parents bless children and children can also bless parents.

Take the time to bless each other with your own words.

May we never lose touch with our blessings.

Sample Opening Ritual for a *Resilience of the Soul* Meeting

Instructions

1. Begin with a *niggun* appropriate for the discussion.
2. You might follow the *niggun* by reading some or all of the following excerpts:

The purpose of all prayer is to uplift the words,
To return them to their source above.
The world was created by the downward flow of letters:
Our task is to form those letters into Words
And take them back to God.
If you come to know this dual process,
Your prayer may be joined to the Constant flow of Creation
Word to word, voice to voice,
Breath to breath, thought to thought.
—Likkutim Y'karim (an early collection of teachings
of the founder of Chasidism, Israel ben Eliezer Baal Shem Tov of Medzibezh
(ca. 1700–1760), and those of his disciples)

Have pre-selected participants read the following:

(Reader 1): We pray to You this day:
(Reader 2): To open our eyes
(Reader 3): To sharpen our understanding
(Reader 4): To gentle our anxiety
(Reader 5): To bring us closer
(Reader 6): To guide our hands and hearts

The words fly upward and come before God.
As God turns to look at the ascending word,
Life flows through all the worlds
And prayer receives its answer.
All this happens in an instant

Adapted from an opening ritual created by Merri Lovinger Arian and Rabbi Shirley Idelson for a course offered at HUC-JIR in New York to rabbinic and cantorial students, entitled "The Art of Creating Meaningful Worship."

And all this happens continually;
Time has no meaning in the sight of God.
The divine spring is ever flowing;
Make yourself into a channel
To receive the waters from above.

—Likkutim Y'karim

Open my eyes, God. Help me to perceive what I have ignored, to uncover what I have forsaken, to find what I have been searching for. Remind me that I don't have to journey far to discover something new, for miracles surround me, blessings and holiness abound. And You are near. Amen.

—*Talking to God,* Naomi Levy[1]

3. This opening ceremony might close with singing the following verse:

עָזִּי וְזִמְרָת יָהּ וַיְהִי־לִי לִישׁוּעָה׃
Ozi v'zimrat Yah, vay ahi-li lishuah.
God is my strength and my might; God is my deliverance. (Psalm 118:14)

For a recording of a *niggun* by Shefa Gold see Rabbi Gold's Web site,
http://www.rabbishefagold.com/OziVZimratYah.html.

---

[1]Naomi Levy, "Talking to God," in *Talking to God: Personal Prayers for Times of Joy, Sadness, Struggle, and Celebration* (New York: Knopf, 2002), p. 31.

For Ourselves and Our Children: A Prayer

We pray for unconditional love,
a love that does not depend on our professional successes,
the perfection of our bodies, or our popularity.

We hope that having experienced that love,
we will be able to give our children such unconditional love—
a love that does not depend on report cards,
beauty, or popularity.

We pray to feel God's acceptance, acceptance of our human frailties as well as our
abilities and virtues.
We pray to believe in a God who can hear and accept all of our feelings, selfish and
selfless, loving and raging.

We hope that having felt that acceptance, we will be able to give our children our
whole-hearted acceptance of their human frailties as well as their abilities and
virtues.
We hope that having found faith in a God who can contain all that we feel, we will
be able to help our children tolerate and manage all of their feelings too.

We pray for permission to grow and to change and to succeed at building lives that
honor God while allowing us to be free to choose our own path.

We hope that having felt such permission we will be able to grant our children
permission to grow and feel free to choose their own path in building lives
independent of us.

Prayer adapted by Rabbi Edythe H. Mencher from a poem by Rabbi Joshua Loth Liebman.

We pray to be aware of God's presence and truth.
We pray to be granted the strength and resilience to find fulfillment in a world in which there are many unforeseen obstacles as well as unexpected entrances to holiness and joy.

We hope to offer our children pathways to sensing God's presence and truth.
We hope to help them to develop the strength and resilience to find fulfillment in a world in which there are many unforeseen obstacles as well as entrances to holiness and joy.

We pray and hope that together we and our children will find sources of hope, strength, and acceptance in one another and in our tradition.

"The Angel of Losses": A Meditation on Loss and Light

The following story, "The Angel of Losses" by Howard Schwartz, a classic Chasidic tale, might be used to initiate a discussion regarding the times when we are overwhelmed by feelings of regret and loss. Young adults, no less than their elders, experience these feelings and we hope the following story, which is not specifically focused on the experience of loss through death, might initiate a discussion about constructive ways to think about loss within the context of our tradition.

"The Angel of Losses"

Late one evening, when Reb Nachman and his Hasidim were gathered together, a strong wind blew in the open window and extinguished all the candles. Some of the Hasidim rose to relight them, but Reb Nachman stopped them, telling them to remain in the dark. So they did. For a long time there was silence. Then one of the Hasidim said: "Tell me, Rebbe, is the blowing out of the candles a good omen or bad?"

"Surely it is a sign that another presence is among us, an angel who watches over us even in the dark. This is *Yodea*, the Angel of Losses. Even now he is watching our lives unfold, recording every detail before it fades. This angel has servants, and his servants have servants. Some of these servants are angels, and some are not. Each of the angels carries a shovel, and they spend all their time digging, searching for losses. For a great deal is lost in our lives.

"So too is every *tzaddik* [a righteous person] a servant of the Angel *Yodea*. That is because even a *tzaddik* who searches after lost things is himself sometimes lost. And as you know, it is necessary to search in the dark, in the realm of the unknown. And with what do you search in the darkness? With the light of the soul. For the soul is a light planted in the *tzaddik* to seek after whatever has been lost.

"What kind of light is it? Not a torch, but a small candle. Yet even so, with it you can search inside deep wells, where darkness is unbroken, peering into every corner and crevice. So for once let us be guided by that light, small though it may be." That is when the Hasidim all saw the flame that was burning before Reb Nachman's face.

Howard Schwartz, "The Angel of Losses," in *Gabriel's Palace: Jewish Mystical Tales* (New York: Oxford, 1993), p. 238.

And even though they were in complete darkness, still they saw his face as if it were glowing in the dark. And indeed it was, for every one of them to see.

★★★

The lifebreath of man is the candle of the Lord.
                                                    —Proverbs 20:27

You're Better Than You Think

A young woman was admitted for treatment because of her heroin addiction. All her veins had become obstructed from injecting herself with narcotics, which resulted in multiple abscesses. This otherwise attractive woman was a pathetic sight because of the many lesions.

In the admission interview she told me that she was a nurse and had easy access to drugs. She had used sedatives for insomnia and Percocet for menstrual cramps. These were taken on her own, not prescribed by a physician. She became addicted to both medications, and when she feared that the hospital would note that drugs were missing, she began using street drugs, eventually gravitating toward heroin. The narcotic habit resulted in her being unable to work, and after using up all her savings, she sold everything, including herself, for money to buy drugs.

I noted that she was wearing a locket, which she said was gold, and asked her why she had not sold it for heroin. She said that it was her mother's and that she would never part with it. I asked her to show it to me. After she handed it to me, I picked up a sharp instrument and acted as if I were about to scratch the locket.

"What are you doing?" she asked with a tone of panic.

"Just scratching this a little bit," I said.

"Why do you want to do that?"

"Oh, it's just something I like to do."

"But that's mine!"

"I know. I will give it back to you."

"But I don't want it all scratched up. It's beautiful, and it's valuable to me."

"You mean that when something has beauty and value, you do not allow it to be marred and ruined?" I asked. Then, taking her hands and showing her the bruises and abscesses, I said, "Do you see what this says? These self-inflicted wounds are a loud statement that says 'I am not beautiful. I have no value.'"

People who do not have a sense of self-worth are prone to do destructive things to themselves or inadvertently allow themselves to be injured. Overcoming self-defeating behavior requires self-esteem. . . . As the young woman's concern for the gold locket indicates, she did not consider herself to be of much value or of any beauty. . . . Sustained recovery from any self-destructive lifestyle requires a change of attitude, one that promotes a positive rather than a negative self-image.

Abraham J. Twerski, *Life's Too Short!: Pull the Plug on Self-Defeating Behavior and Turn on the Power of Self-Esteem* (New York: St. Martin's Press, 1995) pp. 2–3.

When We Feel Lonely: A Prayer

Lord, many are tired and lonely;

Teach us to be their friends.

Many are anxious and afraid;

Help us to calm their fears.

Some are tortured in body and mind;

Imbue them with courage and strength.

Others in their emptiness seek only wealth, fame, or power;

Teach them to value other gifts than these.

Some are drained of faith: they are cynical, bored, or despairing;

Let our faith shine forth for them to see, that through us they

May come to Your love.

And some live with death in their souls: they are stunned, violent,

and filled with hate.

Give us wisdom to save them from the wastelands of the spirit.

Gates of Prayer—The New Union Prayerbook (Central Conference of American Rabbis: New York, 1975), p. 670.

And teach us to show our love; let compassion and knowledge

Combine for the welfare of all your children—

That all may know they are not alone.

A Blessing for
Unconditional Acceptance

נְבָרֵךְ אֶת מְקוֹר הַחַיִּים, שֶׁבָּרָא אֶת צוּרוֹת הַחַיִּים לְמִינֵיהֶן, וְאֶת
כֻּלָּנוּ שְׁלֵמִים, גַּם אִם לֹא מֻשְׁלָמִים.

*Neverekh et mekor hahayyim shebara et tzurot hahayyim leminei-hen, ve'et kulanu shelemim,
gam im lo mushlamim.*

Let us bless the Source of life in its infinite variety, that created all of us whole,
none of us perfect.

Judith Glass, "Afterbirth," in *Lifecycles Volume 2: Jewish Women on Biblical Themes in Contemporary Life*, ed. Debra Orenstein
and Jane Rachel Litman (Woodstock, VT: Jewish Lights, 1998), p. 187.

On God

We believe not in a God of strength but in a fragile light of the spirit that is always threatened by the power of night and that must always be fought for . . .

We believe not in an omnipotent God who will transform the reality closing in around us, which is the given of our lives, but in a God who in a delicate voice calls us from within that reality to break through its hardness and create a resting place for the Divine Presence.

Edward Feld, *The Spirit of Renewal: Finding Faith after the Holocaust* (Woodstock, VT: Jewish Lights, 1991), p. 143.

A Prayer When Feeling Cut Off from God

Dear God,

Open the blocked passageways to you,
the congealed places.

Help us open the doors of trust that have been
jammed with hurt and rejection.

As you open the blossoms in spring,
even as you open the heavens in storm,

Open us to feel your great, awesome,
wonderful presence.

Sheila Peltz Weinberg, "Dear God . . . ," in *Kol Haneshamah: Shabbat Eve*, 2nd ed. (Wyncote, PA: The Reconstructionist Press, 1993), p. 93

On Anger

One cannot always be angry and full of rage, for anger does indeed distract and distort. It can disconnect us from life, as easily as it connects us to life. However, the proper prayer life includes moments of deep anger, as well as times of tranquility and serenity. It includes moments of rage, as well as times of reflection and meditation; moments of sadness, as well as times of gratitude and exultation; "To dwell in the house of [God] forever" together with "For how long, oh [God], for how long shall the wicked rejoice"; "Every breath shall praise God" together with "Oh God make them tumbleweed, as straw before the wind." Psalms, precisely because they flow from the sheer variety of human life, contain the whole range of human emotions, feelings, and awareness—all of them brought before God, all of them incorporated into a full and vital prayer life. One simply alternates, bringing first this and then that feeling before God, turning first this and then that emotion into prayer.[2]

> Praise me, says God, and I will know that you love Me.
> Condemn me, says God, and I will know that you love Me.
> Praise me or condemn Me, and I will know that you love Me.
> Sing out My graces, says God.
> Raise your fist against Me and be angry, says God.
> Sing out graces or express anger,
> Anger is also a kind of praise, says God.[3]

---

[2]David Blumenthal, "Liturgies of Anger," *Cross Currents* 52, no. 2 (Summer 2002): 178–99.
[3]Adapted by Aaron Zeitlin from Toby Landesman, *You Are Not Alone: Solace and Inspiration for Domestic Violence Survivors Based on Jewish Wisdom* (Seattle: FaithTrust Institute, 2004), p. 57.

On Feeling Unworthy

Rabbi Yehoshua ben Levi said: "An entourage of angels always walks in front of people, with a messenger calling out. And what do they say? 'Make way for the image of the Holy One!'" (Midrash—Deuteronomy Rabbah, *R'eih*)

A common malaise which many of us suffer is feeling that we are insufficient or somehow unworthy. It undermines our spirit and our intent and, unfortunately, leads to distress. Judaism teaches that each person is a world unto him- or herself. A Mishnah (Sanhedrin 4:5) expresses this idea by teaching that if we destroy one life it is as of we have destroyed an entire world. What would it take for us to feel worth and uniqueness?

Imagine, if we could actually hear God's angels proclaiming our approach with the words, "Here comes an Image of God." Many of us need such a forthright reminder of our relationship to the Divine. When we walk around with a low sense of self, we deny God's presence in our very being. It is as if we have erased the image of God that resides in our souls. Affirming our inestimable worth can help. When you question yourself, you can stand before a mirror and say, "I am created in the Image of God." If you feel shamed or disregarded, you can say, "I am created in the Image of God and no one can take this fact away from me."

Kerry Olitzky and Lori Forman, from *Sacred Intentions: Daily Inspiration to Strengthen the Spirit* (Woodstock, VT: Jewish Lights, 1999), pp. 311–12.

A Prayer for Those Who Self-Hurt

נִשְׁמַת כָּל-חַי תְּבָרֵךְ אֶת-שִׁמְךָ יהוה אֱלֹהֵינוּ
וְרוּחַ כָּל-בָּשָׂר תְּפָאֵר וּתְרוֹמֵם זִכְרְךָ מַלְכֵּנוּ תָּמִיד.

Nishmat kol chai tevarech et shimcha Adonai Eloheinu ve'ruach kol
basar tefa'er u'tromem zichrecha malkeinu tamid

The soul of every living thing shall bless your name, ETERNAL ONE, but I cannot.
  My soul is hurt within me, my pain too great to utter praise.
God, binder of wounds, healer of broken hearts.
  Sometimes my feelings roil within me like a turbulent sea, confusing me, tossing me in every direction. I am slammed onto the shore but do not reach safety.
  Sometimes I am numb, cut off from my own heart, unable to feel at all, disconnected from all around me. I am stranded on a desert island, lost even to myself.
  Sometimes painful memories sweep over me but I can tell no one of the secret hurts on the inside. I can only mutely show them scars I create on the outside.
  Sometimes I am filled with guilt and shame and am desperate to be rid of the feelings of self-loathing. I hurt myself because it is the only way I know how.

God of the first things and the last, the deity of every creature, who guides the universe in love, all creatures with concern, guide me too in *chesed* and in *rachamim,* in mercy and compassion.

  Help me to find an island of safety and calm as my storm rages, and help others to find me and pull me to safety when I am lost at sea.
  Help my heart of stone to turn to flesh, that I may feel joy *and* sadness, fear *and* relief, that I may have an understanding heart and therefore be joined to the hearts of others.
  Let others notice me where I stand cut off and alone, let others help to draw me in.

Prayer adapted by Rabbi Edythe H. Mencher and Yael Shmilovitz from *Nishmat Kol Chai.*

175

You, God, who wakens all who sleep and stirs all those who slumber, who gives speech to those who cannot speak, who frees the captive and upholds the falling, who makes upright those bent down, do for me, as you have done for them.

Let me find your unconditional love, let me remember your vast ability to forgive, so that I can learn to forgive myself.

Help me too, to love, as do you, the limbs that you have molded for me, the breath and spirit you have breathed into my nostrils, the tongue that you have placed into my mouth, and let all my bones declare: the infinite, I too am a part of you.

Help me today, tomorrow, someday soon to believe that I am worthy of tender touch and love so that I will not lift up my hand in violence against myself again.

בָּרְכִי נַפְשִׁי אֶת־יהוה וְכָל קְרָבַי אֶת־שֵׁם קָדְשׁוֹ

Bar'chi nafshi et Adonai v'chol kravai et shem k'dosho

Bless the ETERNAL, O my soul; let every fiber of my being praise God's holy name.

A Prayer for Those Days When Life Spins Out of Control

When I panic, God, teach me patience.
When I fear, teach me faith.
When I doubt myself, teach me confidence.
When I despair, teach me hope.
When I lose perspective, show me the way—
Back to love, back to life, back to You. Amen

Naomi Levy, *Talking to God: Personal Prayers for Times of Joy, Sadness, Struggle, and Celebration* (New York: Knopf, 2002), p. 29.

A Prayer for the Ability to Pray

Dear God, as I pray, day after unpredictable day,
May the voice of my soul spring forth from my lips.
May I turn to You, God, in tears, in laughter, and in song.
And may my prayers be answered. Amen.

Naomi Levy, *Talking to God: Personal Prayers for Times of Joy, Sadness, Struggle, and Celebration* (New York: Knopf, 2002), p. 31.

A Parent's Prayer for Patience

When my child tests me, teach me, God, how
   to respond with wisdom.
When I grow irritable, send me patience.
When my fury rages, teach me the power of
   restraint.
When I become fixed in my ways, teach me to be
   flexible.
When I take myself too seriously, bless me with a
   sense of humor.
When I am exhausted, fill me with strength.
When I am frightened, fill me with courage.
When I am stubborn, teach me how to bend.
When I act hypocritically, help me to align my
   deeds with my values.
When mundane pressures threaten to overwhelm
   me, help me to remember how truly blessed I
   am.
When I lose my way, God, please guide me on the
   road back to joy, back to love, back to peace,
   back to you. Amen.

Naomi Levy, *Talking to God: Personal Prayers for Times of Joy, Sadness, Struggle, and Celebration* (New York: Knopf, 2002), p. 93.

A Prayer for Bestowing Love Wisely

Love is a great blessing I have to offer.
　　Help me, God, to give my child a love that
　　nourishes and heals.
A love that soothes and comforts.
A love that is steady and eternal.
A love that is free from judgment and conditions.
A love that does not seek to smother or control.
A love that respects my child's needs.
A love that instills confidence and independence,
　　that sets boundaries and limits.
A love that is expressed not by spoiling my child
　　with tangible gifts, but by offering up things
　　that can never be measured:
　　　　my attention, my affection, my creativity,
　　　　my heart.
Thank You, God, for filling me with the capacity
　　to feel and express this holy emotion.
May I love wisely and generously. Amen.

Naomi Levy, *Talking to God: Personal Prayers for Times of Joy, Sadness, Struggle, and Celebration* (New York: Knopf, 2002), p. 95.

A Blessing for a Parent to Say to a Child

May all the gifts hidden inside you find their
   way into the world,
May all the kindness of your thoughts be
   expressed in your deeds,
May all your learning lead to wisdom,
May all your efforts lead to success,
May all the love in your heart be returned to you,
May God bless your body with health and your
   soul with joy,
May God watch over you night and day
   and protect you from harm,
May all your prayers be answered.
Amen.

Naomi Levy, *Talking to God: Personal Prayers for Times of Joy, Sadness, Struggle, and Celebration* (New York: Knopf, 2002), p. 97.

A Prayer for the Parent of a Teenager

My little boy has grown into a man–child. I
don't know how to be his father, God. Sometimes
he wants me, especially when he needs me.
Other times he looks at me with eyes of contempt.

Help me, God, Help me to be patient when
he tests me. Steady me when my temper flares.
Remind me that he still needs me even when he
doesn't want me.

Teach me how to hold him close and let him go,
how to protect him from the world and expose him
to the world, how to guide him and trust him.
Give me strength, God, and confidence, and wisdom.

Watch over him, God. Protect him from those
who can lead him astray. Teach him to believe in
himself, to have faith in goodness. Give him
courage, God, and humility, and happiness, and the
love of good friends.

Bless our family, God, with health, with peace,
with joy, and with love. Amen.

Naomi Levy, *Talking to God: Personal Prayers for Times of Joy, Sadness, Struggle, and Celebration* (New York: Knopf, 2002), p. 108.

A Prayer When a Child Is in Trouble

My child is in trouble, God, and I'm not sure
what to say to her. She needs me now, and I
can't seem to do or say the right thing. Every time I
open my mouth we end up in a fight.

I love her more than life, God; I don't mean to
push her away. I simply don't know how to help her
anymore. When she was small, she would run to
me in tears and I could kiss away her hurts. But
now her hurts run deep, and she shuts me out.

Help her, God. Save her from the grip of those
who are leading her astray. Watch over her, God;
protect her from all harm. Turn her heart to me,
God; help her see that I am not the enemy. Help
me see that she is not my enemy either.

Help me, God. Put insight in my heart and
wisdom on my lips. Let me say the right words of
guidance.

Bless our family, God; grace us with peace.
Amen.

Naomi Levy, *Talking to God: Personal Prayers for Times of Joy, Sadness, Struggle, and Celebration* (New York: Knopf, 2002), p. 109.

A Blessing for Children to Say to Their Parents

You gave me my life. You give me your wisdom,
your guidance, your concern, your love. You
are my mentor, my protector, my moral compass,
my comfort. There are no words to express my
gratitude for all the blessings you have given me.
Still I tell you, thank you.

May God bless you as you have blessed me,
with life, with health, with joy, and with love.
Amen.

Naomi Levy, *Talking to God: Personal Prayers for Times of Joy, Sadness, Struggle, and Celebration* (New York: Knopf, 2002),
p. 113.

Section 7

Resources

Books

Address, Richard. *Refuat HaNefesh Caring for the Soul: A Mental Health Resource and Study Guide.* New York: URJ Press, 2003.

Address, Richard, Joel L. Kushner, and Geoffrey Mitelman. *Kulanu: All of Us: A Program and Resource Guide for Gay, Lesbian, Bisexual, and Transgender Inclusion, Revised and Expanded Edition.* New York: URJ Press, 2007.

Address, Richard and Marcia Hochman. *Litapayach Tikvah: To Nourish Hope Eating Disorders, Perceptions and Perspectives in Jewish Life Today.* New York: Union of American Hebrew Congregations, 2002. *To order, please contact the Department of Jewish Family Concerns.*

Adelman, Penina, Ali Feldman, and Shulamit Rheinharz. *The JGirl's Guide: The Young Jewish Woman's Handbook for Coming of Age.* Woodstock, VT: Jewish Lights Publishing, 2005.

Alderman, Tracy. *The Scarred Soul: Understanding & Ending Self-Inflicted Violence.* Oakland: New Harbinger Publications, 1997.

Bernard, Bonnie. *Resiliency: What We Have Learned.* San Francisco: WestEd, 2004.

Doades, Joanne. *Parenting Jewish Teens: A Guide for the Perplexed.* Woodstock, VT: Jewish Lights, 2007.

Doherty, William J. *Putting Family First: Successful Strategies for Reclaiming Family Life in a Hurry-Up World.* New York: Owl Books, 2002.

Fairburn, Christopher. *Overcoming Binge Eating.* New York: Guilford Press, 1995.

Favazza, Armando. *Bodies under Siege: Self-Mutilation and Body Modification in Culture and Psychiatry.* Baltimore: Johns Hopkins University Press, 1996.

Giannetti, Charlene, and Margaret Sagarese. *The Roller-Coaster Years: Raising Your Child Through the Maddening Yet Magical Middle School Years.* New York: Broadway Books, 1997.

Gordon, Sol. *When Living Hurts,* Revised Edition. New York: URJ Press, 2004.

Haas, Elson, *The Staying Healthy Shopper's Guide: Feed Your Family Safely.* Berkeley, CA: Celestial Arts, 1999.

Kindlon, Dan. *Raising Cain: Protecting the Emotional Life of Boys.* New York: Ballantine Books, 1999.

Kingsonbloom, Jennifer, Karen Conterio, and Wendy Lader. *Bodily Harm: The Breakthrough Treatment Program for Self-Injurers.* New York: Hyperion, 1998.

Lamm, Maurice. *The Power of Hope.* New York: Fireside Publishing, 2005.

Levenkron, Steven. *Cutting: Understanding and Overcoming Self-Mutilation.* New York: Norton, 1998.

Margel, Douglas L. *The Nutrient-Dense Eating Plan: Enjoy a Lifetime of Super Health with This Fundamental Guide to Exceptional Foods.* Laguna Beach, CA: Basic Health Publications, 2005.

Mogel, Wendy. *The Blessing of a Skinned Knee: Using Jewish Teachings to Raise Self-Reliant Children*. New York: Scribner, 2001.

Moore, Judith. *Fat Girl: A True Story*. New York: Hudson Street Press, 2005.

Normandi, Carol Emery, and Laurelee Roark. *It's Not about Food: Change Your Mind; Change Your Life; End Your Obsession with Food and Weight*. New York: Grosset/Putnam, 1999.

Olpin, Michael, and Margie Hesson. *Stress Management for Life: A Research-Based Experiential Approach*. Belmont, AZ: Wadsworth, 2006.

Perlstein, Linda. *Not Much Just Chillin': The Hidden Lives of Middle Schoolers*. New York: Farrar, Strauss, and Giroux, 2003.

Pipher, Mary. *Reviving Ophelia: Saving the Selves of Adolescent Girls*. New York: Putnam, 1994.

———. *The Shelter of Each Other: Rebuilding Our Families*. New York: Ballantine Books, 1996.

Rosenfeld, Alvin, and Nicole Wise. *The Over-Scheduled Child: Avoiding the Hyper-Parenting Trap*. New York: St. Martin's Press, 2000.

Seaward, Brian Luke. *Managing Stress: A Creative Journal*. Boston: Jones and Bartlett, 1994.

Seaward, Brian Luke. *Managing Stress: Principles and Strategies for Health and Well-Being*. Sudbury, MA: Jones and Bartlett, 2004.

Simmons, Rachel. *Odd Girl Out: The Hidden Culture of Aggression in Girls*. New York: Harcourt, 2002.

Sonna, Linda. *The Everything Tween Book: A Parent's Guide to Surviving the Turbulent PreTeen Years*. Avon, MA: Adams Media, 2003.

Strong, Marilee. *A Bright Red Scream: Self-Mutilation and the Language of Pain*. New York: Viking, 1998.

Zailckas, Koren. *Smashed: Story of a Drunken Girlhood*. New York: Viking, 2005.

Movies

Middle School Confessions. Directed by Ellen Goosenberg Kent. Los Angeles: Home Box Office, 2002. (See: **www.hbo.com/schedule** for air dates.)

Smashed: Toxic Tales of Teens and Alcohol. DVD. Directed by Karen Goodman and Kirk Simon. Los Angeles: Home Box Office, 2004. (See: **http://www.radd.org/cwo/ SMASHED/Plan_a_SMASHED_Screening/?preview=yes**.)

Taking Risks & Peer Pressure. DVD. Atlanta: CWK Network. (See: **http://www. mediatechnics. com/mediashop/** Title Search: Taking Risks.) A series of five DVD's dealing with teen driving, the dangers of technology, making healthy choices, and more.

Teen Truth: An Inside Look at Bullying and School Violence. DVD. Directed by Erahm Christopher. Scotts Valley, CA: CustomFlix, 2006.

Popular Movies to Stimulate Conversation

Pump up the Volume. DVD. Directed by Allan Moyle. Los Angeles: New Line Home Video, 1999.

Mean Girls, special ed. DVD. Directed by Mark Waters. Los Angeles: Paramount, 2004.

Thirteen. DVD. Directed by Catherine Hardwicke. Los Angeles: 20th Century Fox, 2004.

Clueless, special ed. DVD. Directed by Amy Heckerling. Los Angeles: Paramount, 2005.
Stand By Me, special ed. DVD. Directed by Rob Reiner. Los Angeles: Sony Pictures, 2000.

Curricula

Love: All That and More: A Video Series and Six-Session Curriculum on Healthy Relationships. **http://www.faithtrustinstitute.org/**.
Love Shouldn't Hurt: Building Healthy Relationships for Jewish Youth. Produced by Shalom Bayit. Oakland, CA. **http://www.faithtrustinstitute.org/**.
Sacred Choices: Adolescent Relationships and Sexual Ethics. New York: URJ Press, 2006. **http://urj.org/youth/sacredchoices/index.cfm?**
Steiner-Adair, Catherine, and Lisa Sjostrom. *Full of Ourselves: A Wellness Program to Advance Girl Power, Health, and Leadership.* New York: Teachers College Press, 2006.
Yad B'Yad: Working Hand in Hand to Create Healthy Relationships. A Curriculum for Grades 6–8. By Irit Eliav. **http://www.faithtrustinstitute.org/**.

Additional Resources

Group Exercises for Enhancing Social Skills and Self-Esteem. By Sirinam S. Khalsa.
Talk with Teens about Self and Stress: 50 Guided Discussions for School and Counseling Groups. By Jean Sunde Peterson and Pamela Espeland.
The Jed Foundation. **http://jedfoundation.org**.
Ulifeline. **http://ulifelife.org/main/home.html**.

Notes

Notes

Notes

Notes

Notes

Notes

Notes

For more information on the Resilience of the Soul
program, including additional resources, please visit the
Department of Jewish Family Concern's Web site at
www.urj.org/jfc/resilience.